Raising
Children

Raising Children

Linda Raney Wright

Tyndale House Publishers, Inc.
Wheaton, Illinois

Coverdale House Publishers, Ltd.
London, England

To my family:
Mr. and Mrs. Ralph Raney
Tom and Barbara Raney
Bill Raney
Ginger and Jerry Bohlken
Brent, Lisa, and Matthew
and to my husband, Rusty Wright

ACKNOWLEDGMENTS

I want to express my gratitude to these friends who helped me in the planning and preparation of this book: Dr. Sherwood E. Wirt, Mrs. John Fain, Miss Jackie Hopping, Mrs. Naomi Hunke, Grace Evans, Mrs. Michael Hopping, and Kathleen Santucci.

In addition, I want to thank all of the women who have shared their lives and experiences in this book for the sake of mothers everywhere.

CONTENTS

Introduction

As a young woman soon to be married, I have taken it upon myself to compile a book about well-known women who have "majored" in rearing children. Though many may have university degrees and some are prominent public speakers or wives of famous men, their distinction as mothers is that they have been personally taught by the great teacher, Jesus Christ.

As I traveled about the country asking questions of parents, it occurred to me that many people have little sensitivity to the spiritual dimensions of rearing children. Approaches to parenthood based on modern psychology generally leave God out. It became apparent to me that godly children can be reared only by godly parents. The best that humans can do, on their own, is to replicate other humans.

I also realized that there were no pat answers on the spiritual level. The same Scripture that "works" on one child and sends him soaring toward spiritual growth may boomerang on another child who isn't ready for that particular emphasis. For this reason the women interviewed here have sensed their need for moment-by-moment wisdom from God. Only he knows how to fit a square peg into a round hole.

I found that families everywhere need the grace of God. Even the most spiritual parents must at times avail themselves of God's "unmerited favor." Our loving heavenly Father is eager to take our mistakes and work them into blessings.

One
Millie Dienert

If you were to ask Millie Dienert why she understands the adolescent so well, she would probably reply, "It's because I was totally an adolescent myself." In those rebellious teenage years, Millie seemed to go the full scale of reacting to her parents.

The only child of a minister in Pennsylvania, Millie was well disciplined, particularly in the significant years between one and eight. She recalls a strong, disciplinarian father, filled with love but firm in his dealings with her. One of her most vivid moments with her dad came at age six.

It was her parents' custom to seat Millie alone on the front pew each Sunday morning at church. Millie's mom sat in the next pew behind her, and her dad was in the pulpit (he could keep an eye on his daughter while he preached). One morning Millie found a little girlfriend to sit with her, and together they had a time of it. Several pews back, the congregation could hear two dwarf-sized parishioners chatting and passing notes as a disgruntled father glanced pointedly from the rostrum, and an annoyed mother laid a firm hand on Millie's shoulder from the back.

Millie Dienert and her husband, Fred, live in Philadelphia, Pennsylvania. Evangelist Billy Graham, father-in-law of one of the three Dienert children, has called Millie the leading Christian women's speaker in America.

But with her strong-willed temperament such measures were not enough. Millie was feeling quite secure knowing that her mom and dad were helpless during church.

She was in for a surprise. Halfway through the sermon her father stopped and addressed the congregation. "I've been speaking to you lately on the importance of rearing a Christian family. And before I speak further I have to take care of my own. My daughter is acting up in the front row. So if you will excuse me, I have a responsibility to take care of."

With that he stepped down from the pulpit, took his daughter by the hand, marched her up the middle aisle and out the back door, pulled her over his knee, and gave her a firm hand-to-bottom routine. When repentance was reached, he marched her again to the front pew and returned to his pulpit to finish his discourse.

Needless to say, Millie behaved better in church after that. But her strong-willed disposition pursued her through puberty and into college years. "I grew up a preacher's kid," says Millie, "and I saw all the inconsistencies and behind-the-scenes lives of many of the Christian leaders in our church. Like many of my friends, I got my eyes on the people instead of the Lord. Resentment and rebellion resulted."

A Christian parent could easily make big mistakes in this period of a daughter's life. But fortunately for Millie God gave her a wise father, who kept communication open and honest with his daughter. "Through all my rebellious years I could tell my father exactly what I felt." Her father, with prayerful diligence, maintained his composure. And Millie entered his room at all hours of the day or night to express her hostility and frustrations to his understanding ear.

Millie recalls today that it is important for a parent to help the child through the difficult teen-age years. "Just because a youth goes through a period of resentment and defiance of well-defined norms and standards does not mean that he will end up a loser in life. I believe that adolescence is a time when a person tests the things they've been taught all their life. They must find out for themselves what they believe and why."

Composed and available through this period of his daughter's life, Millie's father must have sought God zealously for clues in handling his active, party-loving, curiosity-seeking daughter. Millie remembers one situation when she was a member of the Zeta Tau sorority at the University of Pennsylvania. A church member's son made a report of Millie's misconduct to her father. "Every bit of it was true." Yet she received no threats from home. Her father suggested no temporary measures of discipline to keep himself looking good before his parishioners. Instead, he prayed.

A few days later Millie received a telephone call from home. "How are you doing, Millie?" her dad asked. "Your mother and I have been concerned about you. And we just called to let you know that we are praying for you."

"How I wished that Dad had beaten me or thrown some sharp words my way. But he would leave me always with the conviction of his sure love and a reminder that I was committed to the Lord. It was always difficult after that to continue in my wild kind of living."

During these years a carload of her friends were killed in an accident. This caused her to think more deeply and later, make a genuine commitment to Christ.

"Dad's prayers were being answered. Even people who are not outwardly rebellious, if you talk to them for a while, will admit that they have certain misgivings or questions about life. Often these problems may be carried for years without any sign of disagreement or open revolt." Millie remembers one instance where a mother of four came up to her at a retreat. "I don't know what's wrong with me. I'm beginning to question things I've believed all my life."

"So you see," says Mrs. Dienert, "a rebellious period is bound to come to all of us at one time or another." This is why Millie feels it is so important to keep contact with the young adolescent. One of her own daughters, the eldest one, did not have the reaction pattern that her mother had. Her rebellion consisted of hibernating and becoming a recluse from the family. She would walk home from school, and without saying a word to anyone, turn the record player up and remain isolated most of the evening.

"A child needs a parent more at this time than any other time in life," says Mrs. Dienert. And she suggests several ideas that may aid a parent in coping with the adolescent.

"First, keep a wholesome attitude toward the teen-age years. See it as a time every youth must go through." When the young person seeks time to himself, when he decides to disagree, when he marches from the room spouting outlandish or unworkable ideas about life, don't insist that he see all things your way immediately. Give him time and room to work things out.

"Teen-agers have genuine problems they need to work through," says Millie. "They probably don't even know what is bothering them most of the time. Be understanding, and don't take their inconsistencies personally."

"Second," says Millie, "assure the youths that you love them, even though you disagree with some of the things they think or do. Be verbal about it. 'It's so great to have a fine daughter like you; I was just telling a neighbor today how proud we are of you, son; I know you're going through a difficult period right now, dear, but remember we love you dearly; you know, you're really special.' These are phrases that should be used often."

Third, practice togetherness. Many parents send their kids away to summer-long camps, and have separate vacations from the children. But the Dienerts have found that family unity was enhanced through tribe-oriented vacations. "If the vacations are exciting and appealing to the youth, more than likely they will want to join the family for them."

Fourth, Millie reminds parents not to pour the child into their own mold. "Many parents feel they want their child to be what they themselves always wanted to be." But God may have an altogether different plan for the child, not only in vocation, but in temperament and personality as well.

Last, parents should be honest with the youths about their own failings. "There's not a home without moments of stress due to a clash of personalities. It's easy for a parent to react in the wrong way." Mother may lose her temper or have an unkind attitude. At this point she should go to the child and say, "I was wrong. I didn't treat you as I should. Will you forgive me?"

Millie recalled an incident when her youngest girl, Marilyn, was four. Marilyn had a temperament much like Millie's, extrovertish and strong-willed. And so one autumn day the two of them clashed strongly. The little girl was constantly and firmly disciplined for misbehavior. Then shortly before dinner she made up her mind that she'd had all a small child could handle. Her mother heard noises coming from the hall. She turned to see her determined child pulling a suitcase twice her size behind her down the stairs.

"Where are you going?" asked Mrs. Dienert.

"I'm leaving home," retorted Marilyn.

"Why?" questioned Millie.

"I'm going to live with Mrs. Johnson next door. She loves me. She doesn't have any little girls. She will love me."

"Don't you think you are loved?"

"No," snapped the four-year-old. "You've been very nasty to me and I'm leaving."

As Millie looked on with curiosity, Marilyn dragged her suitcase to the front door. It was already dusk and this little child had always feared the dark. Millie decided to play along with her at this point.

"Be sure to call me and let me know how you like your new mother and new home," she teased.

Marilyn looked up and didn't answer. Then her big blue eyes surveyed the situation again. The cold night was approaching outside, and Mommy and warmth were inside. With lowered eyes she announced, "I think I'll go tomorrow."

This little episode at first struck Millie as one of those situations which the child would soon forget. But as she watched her daughter, something alerted her that perhaps the event was more serious. Even though the discipline was normal routine for the day, something Millie thought necessary, still it had registered very wrongly with the child. And so Mrs.

Dienert sat on the stairs and put her arms around Marilyn.

"Mother is very sorry if she has got you to the point where you want to leave home."

Tears welled up in her little daughter's eyes. "Are you really sorry, Mommy?"

"Yes," said Millie.

"Well," she sighed, "I'm sorry too."

"I believe that incident had a lot to do with the years that followed. Marilyn was a lot like me as a teen-ager," says Millie. "And I feel that some of the rapport maintained with her through those years dated back to that day. Marilyn still hasn't forgotten it. In fact she often brings it up.

"Try to evaluate a situation for its future worth. Is it important to prove yourself constantly right in the child's eyes? Or is it better that he realizes that the best of parents can fail? I think that how we accept our failures in life determines what kind of person we become. To acknowledge them and forgive ourselves is to present a healthy attitude to the child. But if we give the image that we are perfect Christians and never make mistakes, we have presented ourselves and the Christian walk erroneously."

It's important that a mother be able to say, "I shouldn't have done that. I made a wrong decision." This should be done directly as a parent deals with a child. And it can be done indirectly as well. "Children always suffer," Millie comments, "when they see only one side of a situation. And so as conversations come up at the dinner table about certain individuals it can be helpful to see that the best of Christians have human weaknesses. However at this point a parent should use discretion and encourage their children to pray for the shortcomings of others rather than to criticize them.

"Because no Christian is always on the mountaintop, parents can also present the realism of the Christian life through their prayer times with the children—the mother confessing to God her failures through the day; the children hearing her tell of her desire to follow Christ, and sensing her attitude of humility as she openly tells the Lord, 'I just cannot live the

Christian life in my own strength, Lord. You will have to live it through me.'"

This honest approach to Christian living helps release the child to open up about his own flounderings. Millie cites one occasion where Marilyn had been deceptive. She had asked her parents for permission to go for a college weekend with her boyfriend, and the Dienerts had insisted she not go. But Marilyn went anyway, leaving home under the pretense that she was going somewhere else.

Because this mother lived close to the Lord, she was sensitive enough to her daughter and to the situation that she knew where Marilyn really was. "If a mother has learned to walk and communicate with the Lord, he tells her many things. No one else has to tell her." And so Millie took her daughter to prayer, asking God to teach her a lesson from the ordeal.

When Marilyn returned home, Millie was not too sure how to approach her disobedient offspring. "It was important that I not get angry or nasty, and yet I couldn't think of an opener to confront my daughter with the subject." "God, show me what to do," she prayed.

A few days later Millie went to Marilyn's room and suggested they have a time of prayer together. This was a natural situation since it was family habit to pray with one another. And Millie decided to use this prayer time as a launching pad to truth. "Lord," Mrs. Dienert prayed in front of Marilyn, "you know that I have tried to deceive you many times. But I have only deceived myself and those around me. Help me and all of us to realize that there is never anyone who has lived so perfectly that they have never wanted to be deceptive. And in the end we can only hurt ourselves."

Millie couldn't see the questioning look arising on Marilyn's face, but over the next few days she was aware that her daughter had gotten the message. Finally two weeks later Mrs. Dienert felt it was time to bring the subject up.

"Marilyn, you know that I know where you spent the weekend a few weeks ago, don't you?"

"Yes, Mother," said Marilyn.

Any defense seemed nonexistent, and mother and daughter were able to discuss openly what Marilyn had done. Finally Marilyn started to cry. "Mother, I had the most miserable weekend of my life."

And Millie couldn't resist her reply. "Marilyn, I'll tell you why you were unhappy there. I knew where you were and I was praying that God would convict you."

Here is proof that honesty, along with God's timing in a situation, can bring issues to the surface. It also shows to the child a real God working amid his or her problems.

Millie tells another incident where the family had to band together in open and honest communication with one another and God. It was in the wee hours of the morning when the headmaster called from Ted's school. He explained to Mrs. Dienert that her fourteen-year-old son had been suddenly taken ill. It came as a complete surprise to Millie, who had talked with Ted the night before and found him in excellent spirits getting ready for the next football game. Ted was sure his team would win.

The news was relayed to Millie that her son was taken ill at eight o'clock that evening. By twelve o'clock he had a fever of 106° and was completely paralyzed. The doctors had diagnosed it as a cross between poliomyelitis and spinal meningitis. And Mrs. Dienert was told that nobody had ever recovered from the disease.

As was often the case in a crisis at their home, Daddy was away on business. The trial fell firmly into Mom's hands. In the darkness of the night Millie felt incapable of handling the situation. At last she called her nine-year-old and sixteen-year-old daughters into the room. "This is one time Mother is not strong," she said. "Many times I have encouraged you and others to believe God. Now, I'm having to fight the battle of faith myself. I am asking myself if I can honestly say, 'Lord, if you want Ted to die or be a vegetable the rest of his life, I am willing.' So you see, girls, what we have to do now is to pray that Mother will pray the right way. You will have to pray for Mother as much as for Ted."

In the days and weeks that followed, this small family banded together, each seeking greater maturity than they had known, and each more sharply conscious of their need for God and one another. The end result of the period of difficulty was joyful. Ted completely recovered. A fearful family renewed its faith. God received great praise.

Later, Millie overheard her daughters telling friends how God had worked a miracle in their brother's life. As she listened she knew they had learned a lesson about God's power and concern that they would never forget. But also she realized that someday two adult women could have an open and honest relationship with God, for they had seen weakness and unbelief in their mother, yet God was faithful to meet her need. "You don't have to be a super Christian, on top of it all, all the time, in order to have a life that pleases God. What he wants is for us to come just as we are. We bring our fears, our doubts, our confusion, right up to the throne of grace. And there God seeks to bless us and give us abundantly of his love."

Millie has one other situation to share in hopes of emphasizing that "honesty is the best policy." It is common for an older child to feel that Mom and Dad are not as strict with the younger children as they were with him.

"Mother," asserted Darlene, "you are not saying 'no' loud enough to Marilyn. If I had ever done what she did, you know you would have taken care of me."

Millie thought about this remark and then went to Darlene's room to discuss it. "Darlene, you said something I would like to clarify. You said that if you had done the same thing Marilyn did, I would have disciplined you. You know, dear, there were many times that I didn't take care of you either, except on my knees in prayer. But it's possible that I am making a mistake with Marilyn. I am wondering if you would pray with me that I would do the right things with her. We can ask God to give us the right, loving attitude toward Marilyn so we can help her."

This type of honest discussion with her daughter had good results in Darlene, who developed a better, more loving attitude toward her younger sister. Now, Marilyn was Darlene's personal prayer concern.

"Of course all these illustrations prove one thing, that we need an expert when it comes to family rearing. And the only expert I know is the One who planned families in the first place. A woman needs to commit her life to the One who created families and has the perfect plan for them. But it's not a life commitment; it's a moment-by-moment commitment. Because family living is a constant intermingling of personalities, a mother must live in vital communication with this Expert in order to solve the riddles of family involvement."

One morning the Dienerts gathered around the breakfast table and sergeant Millie began asking all of those breakfast questions. "All right, Darlene, where is your homework?" "Ted, what did you do with your jacket?" "Marilyn, why don't you finish what's on your plate?" Millie was going through all the hectic minutes that a mother of three has in getting her brood off to school every day.

Right in the middle of the ordeal Marilyn looked up at her mom and said, "Mother, did you pray this morning?" Millie stopped short. "No," she admitted, "I really didn't."

Millie comments that her daughter had a right to question things that morning. For what Marilyn saw was her mother's edginess, irritability, and her fuse that was about to blow. "Actually, I didn't know that Marilyn knew I prayed in the morning. I guess our children know us pretty well." For many years now it has been Millie's practice to set the alarm clock at least fifteen minutes ahead of the rest of the family. And when the buzzer goes off she takes advantage of the extra time for solitude with God in order to prepare herself for her day's activities.

When it comes to a child's extracurricular hours, Millie doesn't try to isolate her children to church-related routines. Rather she encourages them to participate in a wide range of activity. This would include choral groups, journalism, athletics, field trips, student government, junior chamber of commerce, and the like. "The trouble with many of our children," says Millie, "is they are not prepared when they emerge from Christian homes to enter the secular world."

Temptations may be overwhelming if the youth lack awareness and information. Emotional difficulties may result if there has been no preparation for the world's thinking. And also, the young adult reared in a sheltered Christian environment may have a limited witness for Christ.

Perhaps better than shielding the child from encounters with the philosophy and morality of the unbelieving world, the parent should allow careful exposure to it. With the unmasking, an adult can stand close beside the youth with a more mature perspective on the situation. Thus, hopefully, as the young man or woman comes of age, he or she will pursue the Christian life through a knowledgeable personal choice.

Millie encourages parents to be up-to-date on ideas affecting their children. This includes reading the required reading list for school, which will provide hints as to what a child is thinking about. "And it's not good enough to dismiss certain subjects, books, television programs, or viewpoints with 'Well, you just shouldn't talk about it, see it, do it, or read it.' It should be emphasized that only a thorough explanation, pointing out the reasons for the decision, and helping the child understand the why's for himself, will have lasting benefit."

The most important reason for channeling youth into secular activities is that they may have a witness for Christ. Over the years many youngsters were brought into the Dienert home who didn't have the vaguest idea of what Christianity was all about. One of Darlene's closest friends, a Jewish girl, was often involved in discussions at this home about questions of life and death, beliefs, values, and goals. Darlene, Ted, and Marilyn had all learned early of the need for people to know a living Savior, and hence made no apology for such rap sessions.

Their friends weren't cornered or embarrassed, nor did they have the gospel shoved down their throats. But they did observe that this home was different. They prayed before meals and about problems that arose. Their standard of conduct was rooted in wanting to please a loving God. And so when Ted had his lifeguard buddies over from the beach it was never unusual to see big, barefooted men seated in a circle on the living room floor, asking about life's meaning. At times some of them bowed their heads and committed their lives to Jesus Christ. And it was in a similar scene that Darlene's friend found her personal Messiah.

"In opening your home to the children's friends, it's not important that the house is large or the refreshments extravagant. In fact, a round of pretzels is just as meaningful when it is accompanied by love and understanding. Kids look for the welcome mat out and a place where they can kick off their shoes and let down their hair. What's really important is that a home is comfortable and fun."

One other suggestion that many mothers should take note of is that her appearance is important to a child's good feeling about themselves. This doesn't mean that she shops at Saks Fifth Avenue, but it does imply that she is neat and pleasant. Remember, any child wants to turn to friends and say with a sense of pride, "That's my mom."

"It's easy," says Mrs. Dienert, "for children to develop resentment toward their mother, because she is a disciplinary figure and one they test their independence against. But if that mother has tried to keep sharp, 'with it,' and abreast of things, they have to respect her for her efforts." And with God's help, any parents can keep their child's respect if they are determined to do so.

Mrs. Fred Dienert has reared three Christian children. Now she travels and ministers to women all over the world. "How grateful I am to have had the benefit of a godly mother and father as I grew up. It's largely to their faithfulness to Christ that I credit my own walk and service to the Lord. It bears repeating that parents should never give up hope for their children, but continue to commit them into the loving arms of the heavenly Father. He is able to work where even the best human parents cannot."

Two
Arvella Schuller

When Dr. and Mrs. Robert Schuller married they had very clear goals for rearing a family. And along with this they knew just what they wanted in number and gender: two boys and two girls.

For a long time it looked as if this was exactly what they were going to get. First came Sheila, then Robert, then Jeanne. A short time lapse ensued in which the parents saved the boy's clothes for the son who was to follow. A list of all boy's names was being considered for the next child.

When the pregnancy came, excitement mounted. They waited eagerly for the fourth child and second boy. "And that's how Carol came about," laughs Mrs. Schuller.

As soon as they were informed she was a girl, Mrs. Schuller said, "I want to become pregnant again so I can have another boy." Finally, when Gretchen showed up on Valentine's Day, the Schullers decided that God knew best. Their plans had been discarded for a better idea!

When Arvella Schuller looks at her happy home and exciting marriage she bubbles with enthusiasm over the possibilities that are present. When they married, she and her

---

Arvella Schuller is the mother of five. Her husband, Robert, is pastor of Garden Grove (Calif.) Community Church, perhaps the nation's best-known drive-in church. Arvella edited the book Mommy Is Better Than a Blanket.

husband were determined to have a thriving home—a home that would produce children who love God and want to serve him with all their hearts.

When asked what she feels is missing from most Christian homes, Arvella responded, "Positive thinking is missing in Christian homes. The Christian faith is approached on a negative rather than a positive basis. Most things are presented as what a child can't do or can't be, rather than showing all the great possibilities God has in store for him.

"We do say 'no' in our home. We have many family rules that everyone must abide by. We do not smoke and we do not drink. These are obvious rules, yet we do not harp on this fact. Rather our approach is, 'God has given us such fantastic bodies, and God has such an adventurous life ahead for us, that we want to take good care of ourselves so we can experience every exciting minute of it.'"

In regard to TV shows or the wrong kind of movies or radio programs, the Schullers have definite rules. But again the emphasis is not on "We can't allow this" or "You cannot see this."

"That would hurt the wonderful mind God has given you," Robert and Arvella explain to the children. "Everything you see is recorded in your subconscious, developing you into a certain kind of person. You become what you watch and listen to. We want you to watch and listen to the programs that will make you a better person."

There are parties at school that the children are not permitted to attend. When these or other unsuitable activities come up, Mrs. Schuller's first approach is to sit down and explain to the children the why's of her decision. "But then, I tell them that they can invite a few friends into our home, or we will take them out to dinner, or go to Disneyland, or create something that is far more interesting than the activity they are missing.

"A parent shouldn't leave a vacuum in which the Christian child feels that living for God isn't much fun. We can present the perspective, 'For these reasons it's not good that you do this. But it's much better and much more fun to try this.'"

The order of things at this prosperous home is: first, we are Christians; second, we are Schullers. Under the title Christian, the parents instruct the children, "You live as you do because you are a child of God."

But the second rule is that we do such and such because we are Schullers. "We are proud of the way our home is. We want you to be proud of it too!" This is the message these parents transmit to their offspring. "When you are outside of our home you are ambassadors for Christ—and ambassadors for the Schullers. So walk with your head high and represent the Lord and your family as well."

In Robert Schuller's book, *Power Ideas for a Happy Family*, he describes the family as a small town, a tiny state, a mini-nation. In this little nation the husband is the king, the wife the queen, and every son and daughter is a prince or a princess.

"We work very hard at instilling this family pride. We want to leave them with the feeling that 'it's good to be a Christian' and 'it's good to be a Schuller, too.'"

Robert and Arvella believe that it is vital to let children know how individually important they are. In many homes children feel that they are in the way. "But in our home our children are our hobby. They know that Daddy's work comes first. But they are second—and they finish a strong second at home. As parents, we don't run around to friends or clubs. All of our extra time is spent with our children. The only exception is when Robert and I have an evening to ourselves every Monday. We go out to dinner and plan the next seven days."

Many years ago a wise man told Mrs. Schuller, "Never assume! Never assume that either your husband or your children know that they are loved! Instead, tell them constantly of your love—and demonstrate it with great affection."

Affection is another ingredient missing from many Christian homes. "It's important to check and recheck your children's need for love. We tell each other, 'I love you,' often. We put our arms around our children as they leave for school and wish them a good day. At night we give them a kiss and a hug. Certainly love is present in many families, but the important thing is that it not be *assumed* but *assured."*

Arvella and Robert grew up in the same community in Iowa, the children of simple farm families. They attended the same schools, yet did not meet until after college because of four years' difference in their ages. But one Sunday, when Robert was home from seminary, he spoke at the church where Arvella was organist. This guest minister rapidly won her heart, and a year and a half later they were married.

"We think marriage is absolutely the greatest," says Arvella. "We feel that God brought us together to be a team in Robert's ministry and in the rearing of our children. It may surprise some but we seldom make a decision alone. We talk almost everything over together—not only the major decisions, but many of the things that come up in the everyday lives of our children. We make an attempt to discuss problems together and then present our case to the child. The children have heard more than once, 'Wait until your father comes home. This is serious, and your father and I will have to discuss how to handle it.' They do not consider this a threat, but are accustomed to the idea that Mom and Dad are rearing them together."

Perhaps the key word at the Schuller home is *success.* The most emphasized thought is: "God has given us one life to live. We owe it to him to live life with as much success as we can." Another way they phrase this thought is,

> Only one life; 'twill soon be past.
> Only what's done for Christ will last.

The children have been taught since the time they were tiny that they were born with a purpose. God has a job for each of them to do. Success is further defined by the Schullers to their children as not so much what they *do,* but what they *are.*

They have been taught to believe God for big things, that God is interested in fulfilling their every dream. One day Dr. Schuller and his son Robert were riding past a horse ranch.

"Daddy," he said, "I'm going to get me a horse some day."

"Oh," said his dad, "how do you plan to do that? You know preachers don't make much money."

His son snapped back, "Dad, you told me that if I think I can, I can. God will help me. You told me to be a positive thinker. I'm thinking that God will help me get a pony."

"We had a good laugh over this," says Mrs. Schuller, "but we were encouraged that at six years old, a little boy was already developing an optimistic outlook on life. He saw a big God who wanted to meet his needs."

Actually, the Schullers were unable to buy their son a pony. But God had his own way of fulfilling this boy's desire. In his teen years Robert spent summers on his uncle's farm in Iowa. There he had his own personal riding pony.

"We discipline our children for wrong thinking," says Mrs. Schuller. "Dad doesn't permit any critical or resentful or unbelieving attitudes, or any self-pity, in our home. If they occur, a child may get sent to his room, or be induced to apologize, or have to endure a long lecture from his father."

It's natural for a child to pick up negative attitudes about life, about God, and about himself. So at this home there is an enforced rule to keep attitudes filled with faith and love. "If we allow any pessimistic attitudes to creep into our home, it literally destroys our home spirit," says Mrs. Schuller.

"Of course, we realize that the children often have bad days." When they do, Arvella immediately asks "Why? What's wrong?" She lets them get it all out of their system: their complaints, hurts, and problems. Then she encourages them to take the right attitude on the matter. "Look," she says, "you're affecting the whole house with this kind of spirit. Do you want us all to be this way? If everyone in the house acted like you are now, what kind of a home would we have?"

Here again Mrs. Schuller emphasizes to the children that the family is a team, a working group, a mini-nation. Each must work on behalf of the other. "Occasionally we have tape recorded the children in their grumbling moments. And when they have to sit and hear themselves played back, it's enough punishment.

"Of course, positive thinking would be nothing if we didn't have the Lord and his Word to back up our beliefs. I couldn't be a mother without God and faith in God. It's the most important element we can instill in our children.

"Home devotions are the primary way we stimulate faith. We begin the day together with God." It's been the Schuller's practice to have breakfast together every day. The children have never been allowed to take an early morning class at school because from 7:30 to 8:00 A.M. breakfast and devotions are required.

At the table each reviews the verses assigned each week. Then prayer requests are given such as, "Please pray for me. I have a stiff history exam." Dr. Schuller would ask for prayer for a ten o'clock speaking engagement. Robert, Jr., would announce that he had a wrestling match that day he wanted to win.

Then all seven would hold hands around the breakfast table to give their requests to the Lord.

"Of course, when it comes right down to it," says Arvella, "the best way to impart faith to a child is to *live* faith in front of him. A child can see right through phonies. They pick up what our relationship with God and Christ *really* is. And so at our house when things get rough I just explain to the children, 'The only answer I know is God. So we'll just have to stop right now and pray about it.'

"Our most beautiful time with our children is around the dinner table. Here, the person of Christ is often shared with the children. When the children were young we had an extra chair at the dinner table and the children learned that Jesus was right there with us."

At the dinner table many of the children's questions were answered. Dr. Schuller, so resourceful in bringing the children out of themselves, encouraged them that whatever was bothering them they could bring up. Doubts or questions about God and his ways are freely discussed. "We tell them that it's better to discuss any problem than to conceal it. This is the best way to resolve it."

The children love the long talks they have with their dad. Each parent may spend hours talking with one child. They may come into their parents' bedroom and stretch out with Dad on the bed, talking about any kind of subject. But inevitably the conversation ends up on God. Always they stress to the children what a wonderful loving God they have.

They read Bible stories to the children, play Christian records, and watch TV programs together that deal with Christ. "We permit little TV in our home," says Mrs. Schuller, "and no rock and roll music. We find that this noise takes away from the atmosphere we want to project. A child often needs quietness for opportunity to think through the many changes in his life. Too much TV or loud music can be a distraction, an easy escape from a child's problem."

On Saturday night the Schullers have their family night prayer circle. Parents and children pray for Dad's sermon the next morning, for the congregation, for the Sunday school teachers, and for family needs. Then they sing together. "Our family is musical. We love to sing hymns and Christian choruses." They often sing "Surely goodness and mercy shall follow me all the days of my life." They learned this little chorus at a retreat. Since then it has been "our family song." At the last meal they had together before Robert, Jr., returned to college and Sheila left for Europe, they sang it. The children left knowing that wherever they went God's goodness and mercy *would* go with them!

The family has a cabin in the mountains. Many years ago Dr. and Mrs. Schuller found a beautiful site in the mountains and began payments on it. Then when it was finally paid for, they began dreaming about a cabin. As a family they built the house. The children remember how it was planned on paper. Then on many weekends they watched it take form. Each participated, painting and working faithfully on their retreat cabin.

"The cabin means a lot especially to our children, because they know they have Daddy all to themselves. No telephone calls, no appointments, no emergencies. Dad and Mom have time only for them.

"We use the cabin to regroup ourselves as a family. We have picnics, long hikes, and fishing. Often Dad and just one child make a morning of it, giving him time to talk to that one about his relationship with God, or whatever might be troubling him."

Any Christmas there are five Christmas services at the Garden Grove Community Church, where Dr. Schuller preaches. All the children participate, in choir or volunteer work. The children don't resent this because Christmas Day and the week following they have Daddy all to themselves. It could become easy for the children to resent Dad, and God who is employing Dad, if special times weren't set aside especially for them. "They have to know that they aren't in competition with God or Daddy's work. Too many children go wrong because they sense they aren't special to anyone. Our children are very, very important to us and we try to lavish attention on them.

"Sometimes at our mountain cabin we have been snowed in on a Sunday. And instead of Daddy's doing the preaching, the children are required to have their own church service. It's been fantastic to watch them prepare the sermon, find out Bible verses, give the pastoral prayer, and choose their own hymns. I've often been amazed at some of their concepts of worship, a little bit different from what we planned. But we've learned much from our children and from their faith in God."

The children are all enrolled in Sunday school and attend church, but these parents believe that the main place of teaching is not in the church, but in the home. "In our home we teach the Bible, using Bible aids and dictionaries. There are many good Bible records that we also use, especially for the little ones. They include stories of Samson, David and Goliath, and the Boy and Five Fishes. These are very happily presented with songs in a manner that will stick with the child. As for our use of the Scriptures, we try to get the Bible in contemporary versions that are attractive to the children. Along with this we encourage Scripture memorization. As a family we memorize at least one verse a week. But we have also committed entire passages to memory, such as 1 Corinthians 13, and many of the psalms.

"We believe that faith and humor go together, that laughing and good times are important for a balanced Christian home. I don't believe my husband and I could have survived the ministry if it weren't for all the times we learned to laugh. We laugh at our own mistakes and our own stupidity at times. And as we counsel people with broken homes, messed up marriages, or personal problems, we have to keep a sense of humor or the situation gets too much for us.

"We encourage our children to tell happy stories, jokes, and riddles. They often play jokes on each other. On April Fool's Day there's no telling what you will find: something marked toothpaste when it's hair cream, or sugar in the salt shaker, or salt in the sugar bowl."

One day Dr. Schuller moved all the clocks ahead. Then he ran into all the children's rooms yelling, "Get up! Get up! You're late for school!" The children rushed until at the breakfast table he smiled. "April fools!" But he had the hardest time of it. All the children jumped on him, really messing up his hair and tie.

The Schullers have found many ways to have fun. Even if Dad has only a very few moments from one meeting to the next, he'll come in and announce, "Let's play hide and seek." When there's more time together they will pull out a game of Monopoly, Scrabble, Chinese checkers, or chess. Even the little ones take on their Dad in this. The children also work a variety of picture puzzles. In the mountains they love to make snowmen together or go skiing.

Occasionally Mrs. Schuller will use a treat night. One night a special Cinderella program was presented on TV. Dad wasn't home and the oldest children were at choir rehearsal. Mrs. Schuller fixed TV dinners and sat down with Carol and Gretchen to watch the special. This was a big treat for the little ones. Then there are the trips to Farrell's Ice Cream Parlor for a scoop of ice cream in their favorite flavor.

"When faith is a part of living, faith is part of fun times," says Mrs. Schuller. They use these opportunities to encourage their children in their relationship with Christ. "And more than once we've had to burst out laughing at one of our children's requests during prayer time. At church also there is a lot of kidding and teasing. We want our kids to learn that God wants them to have a good time. We don't allow negative humor in our home, the kind that hurts someone else or makes fun of someone else." But otherwise, at the Schuller home, it could often be said at the end of the day, "A good time was had by all!"

In line with a positive outlook Mrs. Schuller doesn't advise that parents spend time thinking about their failures—but to keep their mind on the challenges that lie ahead, trusting God to work through the problems. "With God all things are possible!" is one of the family's favorite Bible verses.

"My greatest regret as a mother is that I don't spend enough time with my children." As each day ends, Mrs. Schuller wishes she could have had more time to enjoy them. She also regrets that children grow up so fast. "I wish I could keep them longer, yet I'm preparing them for a life of their own." A Bible proverb says, "An eagle stirs up her nest so that her young will fly." This verse reminds Arvella to prepare her children for the time that they will be adults.

"We have been very careful not to label our children in any negative way. For instance, when they do fail us in some way, we never label them 'failures' because this may stick with them in their adult years." Dr. Schuller tells the story that when he was at school his English teacher told him he would be a good speaker, but never a good writer. This label in some ways crippled him. For many years he felt he couldn't write. But one day he traced his negative attitude to its origin. Resolving that "I can do *all things* through *Christ,*" he has since written a number of books. "This illustrates that you can hinder a person by labeling him in a negative way."

The Schuller's two youngest daughters are assigned to keeping their bedroom clean. This is one of their responsibilities. Before school and at bedtime mother checks the bedroom, which often looks as if a cyclone has struck. In this situation the children have failed to live up to Mom's expectations. But she is careful not to label them as failures. "I don't say, 'You are *messy* girls.'" Instead she takes a positive approach. She tries to motivate them with, "Your room isn't as pretty as it can be. If you keep throwing your things on the floor like this, it just means you want it to be trash and I'll have to take it to the trash can.

"This motivates them to keep their things on the shelves, yet they haven't been branded as 'disorderly' for the rest of their lives."

Robert Schuller's perspective on failure is refreshing. In his vocabulary and in the biblical perspective there is no such thing as failure for the one who cements his life in Christ. Rather he teaches that when there is a roadblock, an apparent failure, it means that God has a better idea. When things look as if they are at the end of things, it means that it is time for a new beginning. This is what is shared with the children.

"And when trials come," says Mrs. Schuller, "we know that our children feel that we are with them in their crisis. In this way they are more confident that God is with them as well. Since our oldest children have gone to college, our phone bill has been over a hundred dollars a month. This is because we have always taught them that no matter what time of day it was, we were never farther away from them than the telephone. They call home collect, often!"

The oldest daughter, Sheila, after completing four years of college, was denied entrance into ten different medical schools, yet for several years she'd had a goal of becoming a medical missionary. Several years ago she had visited New Guinea with her parents, and felt again that that's where God was calling her for service as a pediatrician.

When Sheila was being rejected by one medical school after another, she would often call home crying. "I just don't know why the doors are closing. I've examined myself; I just know that God wants me to do this. I've prayed about it. I feel so right going into medicine."

"Invariably," says Mrs. Schuller, "a Bible verse would

come into my mind. I would tell her over the phone, 'Now here's a Bible verse for you to hang on to.'"

One time when she called, Sheila said, "I don't know why I wasted four years in chemistry if I can't be a medical missionary." But the Schullers brought their daughter back to the Word of God. It gave her assurance that God had a better plan. What looked like the end of the line was really a new beginning.

Only months after the rejections Sheila was learning that her desire to be a children's doctor was perhaps not so foolproof as she had assumed. She discovered that she had a rich ability to inspire children. And perhaps her true goal wasn't so much healing children as helping children. This young girl needed Mom and Dad to feed her God's perspective from the Word during this trying time.

Sheila's goal of becoming a medical missionary began when she was thirteen years old. This was a result of something Dr. and Mrs. Schuller heard from the principal of the junior high school when their daughter entered. The principal made a statement that a child entering junior high school must have a *goal.* A child without a goal will inevitably get into trouble. They may change the goal, but at least they should have one, he said.

And so the Schullers used this advice. They talked clearly with each child at the point of entering junior high school. They asked them, "What do you want to do? What do you want to be? You have only one life, and we don't want you to waste time and school by taking the wrong courses."

"We believe that helping our children set goals is what has saved them through their teen-age years from drugs, delinquency, and getting into the wrong crowd. Even Sheila, with her change in goals, hasn't had it nearly so rough as if she hadn't had a goal.

"Our fifteen-year-old isn't exactly sure of what she wants to do. She thinks she wants to be a minister of youth. We have talked about this with her and encouraged her in it.

"If the children want to change their goals, we talk about it with them." Their son at thirteen set his goal to be a minister like his father. Then, when he was a junior in high school, for a couple of months he wanted to be a doctor. Then he wanted to be a lawyer because his best friend was going to be a lawyer. "We didn't say too much to him about his change in goals. We did talk it over with him, but we didn't let him know whether we were upset with the decision or not. We just encouraged him to be sure so that he could begin moving in that direction." That same year their son went on a Christian retreat. When he returned home he was again sure that God wanted him to go into full-time Christian work as a minister. There has been no further swerving from that goal, and he is now in college preparing for it.

"We encourage the children to dream." If God is in the center, and the dream involves helping other people, then they can count on the Lord to fulfill it. "We point out their good points. We try to tell them specifically how talented they are in certain areas, such as speaking, singing, or helping others in some way. We tell them, 'This is the gift that God has given you. You must use it!' "

Preparation in reaching the goal is strongly stressed in the Schullers' home. "Our children automatically grew up with the idea that they would attend college. They were told to think about this ahead of time and take courses heading in that direction. And they were encouraged to get involved in activities that would be good preparation in that field. Our son is now studying Greek in hopes of being a well-prepared minister someday."

Along with this all the children had to take music lessons. "We felt that this was very important. It's a good discipline for children. Also if they want to use music in fulfilling their dreams they have the background they need.

"Every child is different and some need to learn patience by waiting for their dreams to be fulfilled. Gretchen, our youngest, is very patient and quiet. But Carol has no patience. If she gets an idea, it has to be carried out immediately. I often say, 'Carol, you must wait for this. You can't have it now.' "

One thing to help children understand patience is to have

them plant things in their own garden where they have to watch and wait for God's timing. They also learn patience by having animals such as rabbits or puppies to raise. Here they see that there is a certain timing in seeing things grow, whether people, animals, dreams, or ideas.

The older children have learned patience from having the little ones around. When the two youngest girls help themselves to her makeup, Sheila needs a great deal of patience. "Patience," Arvella says, "is important for every child to learn, because in the fulfilling of our dreams God often encourages us to wait. His wonderful plan for us takes not only preparation but time.

"Psychologists tell us that each person must have a place. We know that it's significant for our children to know that they have a place in our home, an important place. They definitely belong here. The older children have their own bedrooms. And even though the two younger girls share a room, each has a place in the bedroom that is exclusively her own. Here they put their own clothes, their own toys, and their own keepsakes. Each has a place at the table also. And when we go driving each one has a place in the car.

"I've been a very strict disciplinarian. I've made it a firm rule that when the children are not in school or at a legitimate function that has been approved ahead of time, such as church, sports, choir rehearsal, etc., that their place is at home. I don't allow them to go off and call me from a friend's house, and say 'Mom, I'm at someone's house and I don't know when I'll be home.'

"Of course, I've had some static from my children on this, particularly when they began to drive. They've argued for their freedom. But it has been a stern, unyielding rule here that the parents know where their children are at all times. I tell them, 'I am responsible for you. God has given me this responsibility. When you leave home and are away at school, God and you can make the decisions. But while you are at home, you need to check with Mom and Dad.' If they don't report home they know they'll be put on curfew or grounded for awhile."

Mrs. Schuller believes that if God gives her a responsibility he will hold her accountable for it. So this check on her children's activities is important. Mrs. Schuller has a letter from a young man, age ten, in a book called, *Mommy Is Better Than a Blanket.* This is a selection of letters about mothers which Mrs. Schuller edited. The boy wrote:

> My mother is the meanest mother in the whole world. While other kids are having cookies and candy for breakfast I have to have bacon, eggs, and toast. For lunch while they are having cake and ice cream I have to have sandwiches. You probably know that my dinner was also different from theirs. While other kids were sleeping in on Saturday my mother had to wake us and have us work. The way she treated us you would have thought we were part of the chain gang. When we told her we would be home in an hour she would expect us to be home in one hour and not one minute later. I thank God he gave me the meanest mother in the whole world so I could grow up to be a God-loving obedient child.
>
> The End
> Ken
> Grade 5
> Age 10

Mrs. Schuller knows that "many problems confront a mother today. It's easy to get our attention on messy children, dirty clothes, disorganized schedules, automatic houses that automatically break down! We have our own human weaknesses to contend with. We may feel that our children will grow up to be dropouts and failures.

"And so, it's important that a mother keeps her attention where it belongs—and that is on the Lord. She must know that God is for her. He is for her rearing a successful family. This is his will. And he will back her and help her to do all that's needed in order to assist her in reaching this goal. For *with God, all things are possible!*"

In *Mommy Is Better Than a Blanket,* a little girl writes: "There must be a loving God for my mother is so lovable."

"If my children can grow up," Arvella concluded, "knowing a loving God because they've seen his love in me—then I know that I have succeeded as a mother."

Three
Jeanne Hendricks

When the first child, Barbara, was born to Howie and Jeanne Hendricks in their second year of marriage, Jeanne wasn't quite ready for motherhood. She wanted some time in the workaday world. "God has just intervened and messed up my plans," she thought. A similar problem occurred when she was expecting her second child, Bob.

Later when Bev, the third baby, was coming, Jeanne's resentment was intense. "I remember one day in particular," she says, "when I was lying in bed. I thought, 'Lord why are you doing this to me? I'm not ready for another child, I am just not ready. I'm too busy with two.'"

And the Lord brought into Jeanne's mind, "Look, you have things to learn you don't even *know* you have to learn. And you're trying to tell me you don't need another child? I want you to know that you *do* need another child!"

God soon brought Bev, a bubbly, happy little child, into the Hendricks' life. "Up until that time," says Jeanne, "the four of us were very, very serious people. But little Bev injected a whole new gaiety into our group. This was one of the

Jeanne Hendricks and her husband, Howard, a Dallas Theological Seminary professor, speak and write as a team. They have four children and live in Dallas, Texas. Howard has written two books, Heaven Help the Home *and* Say It with Love.

bombshells God used to teach us that we need not resist his ways. He also knows what is best for us.

"This is what I tell many of the student wives, where Howie teaches. They often come with their husbands to seminary, having their own plans of when to have a family. Of course, it's all right to follow personal convictions on birth control, but don't forget to figure God in the equation. He may have better plans."

The Lord constantly points out to Jeanne that she learns more from her children than her children learn from her. Just prior to the birth of Bob, the Hendricks were living in a house trailer. Howie was a seminary student and the baby was due just before his graduation. Because the housing situation was tight, they were unable to get the apartment they had signed up for months before. And in the trailer there was not space for even a squirrel's nest, let alone another baby.

Jeanne kept telling the Lord, "I have to get out of here. You've got to find us a place to live." The day came when the baby was due and the Hendricks were still in the trailer. Jeanne was panicky. Two days later the baby came. By the time she returned from the hospital, the family was completely moved into a new apartment. "The Lord had arranged it so that I wouldn't have to get stuck with the moving," says Jeanne. "He allowed this to prove to me again that I didn't need to worry about provisions." And God continued to test Jeanne, to build her faith in his perfect plan.

In the pastorate Jeanne soon discovered the loneliness of leadership. It wasn't appropriate to share too many personal problems with people in the congregation. "I was shut up to the Lord," says Jeanne, "and was amazed to find that he was more than adequate."

Jeanne has developed a good relationship with God. She's honest and verbal to him about everything. "I'm just simpleminded enough to believe that the Lord is interested in every detail of my life. In other words, I believe that what interests me interests him too."

Howie and Jeanne met in their teens when Howie was a

favorite song leader in Philadelphia. He arranged for friends to get Jeanne to the station when he left on a train to Wheaton College. There he asked her if he could write to her. "I was appalled," said Jeanne, "to receive a lengthy letter only days after he left." And thus correspondence began a dating relationship that lasted for five years.

Both Howie and Jeanne entered marriage with the determination to have a Christian home. Howie made a request of the Lord before he married. He didn't care whether God would give him a worldwide ministry or success in other areas, but he wanted God, above all else, to give him a Christian home. "We haven't always had an example of a perfect home," says Jeanne, "but we are well motivated. We've done a lot of studying and thinking about what God wants from us." And considering this attitude, it's not surprising that their four grown children are all actively involved in Christian things today.

"Many people have asked us why our children have gone in this Christian direction. I believe that it's more than example. My husband and I have *enjoyed* being in a ministry. The children's father has an exuberance when he talks about his work, and I believe that the children have caught this spirit of excitement and adventure.

"But also, we have never, never forced a Christian ministry on our children. Other people outside of the home have made comments like, 'Aren't you going to be a preacher like your dad?' But the children have been well prepared by us. We repeatedly told them that, 'We want you to do whatever God wants you to do. If it's a salesman, or a garbage man, or a missionary, we will be happy knowing you are in the center of God's will!' "

Not only with vocation but with so-called Christian mores, Mrs. Hendricks tried not to push her children. "Many children of parents in Christian vocations are handicapped because it's always thrown up to them that they should or should not do something because of who their parents are." When church people suggested a certain behavior for one of their children, Jeanne would reply, "Look, my children are just normal children. They are going to do the same things and make the same mistakes as other children."

And to the children she would reiterate that what was important was not that they conform to standards in the Christian community, but that, in their hearts, they sought to do the will of God. "We do—or do not do—something for one basic reason: because it's pleasing or displeasing to the Lord. It makes no difference what your father does for a living. Our lives are to be lived for Christ because he loved us and died for us."

One thing the Hendricks are well prepared to discuss is the teen-age years. They have been successful with their children in spite of pressures toward drug use and immorality in their community.

First, Jeanne says, a parent should verbalize care and love for the child often. Let them know that you really are trying to help them.

Second, Jeanne recommends that a parent "cooperate with nature." Every child is different and has a different bent. A mother needs to study him to know him. Then cooperating with his age, temperament, and personality, you guide him. It's like growing a plant. Some plants need more water, some need more sunshine. In the same way, look for what works best with each of your children.

Bob was very sensitive as a young person. One evening, when his mom came in to tuck him into bed, he said, "I don't want you to kiss me good-night. That's kid stuff."

"Okay," said Mom. She gave Bill, her younger boy, a kiss, and then went out of the room. Every night thereafter Jeanne would go into the room, kiss Bill, and pat Bob on the leg as she said good-night.

"This went on for months," Mrs. Hendricks said, "because I seemed to realize that Bob wasn't able to handle that particular emotion at that time."

Then one night, many months later, she went to tuck in the boys. As she was kissing Bill she heard a tiny, high-pitched voice from the top bunk—a voice that was just beginning to change: "Mom, you missed somebody up here." And so, without any comment which would draw attention to her son's change of attitude, Jeanne reached up and gave her oldest boy an affectionate hug and kiss. She said good-night and left the room.

"This is what I mean by cooperating with nature," said Jeanne. "Growing up is difficult for any child, particularly at the age when a girl's body begins to develop and womanly changes come; or when a boy's voice begins to change and he takes on manly characteristics. They are so easily embarrassed about themselves and the new feelings they are having inside."

A mother who knows when to discuss a matter or leave it privately for a child to work out himself is a blessing to any adolescent. "And when you learn to know your child, and respect his inmost feelings, you will know how to cooperate with nature.

"It is particularly important that a mother doesn't take offense at these reactions. My son didn't know how to handle his own emotions. He was only doing what he knew to do."

The same idea of cooperating with nature needed to be applied when Bob was struggling with the impersonal coldness of his large city school. He often felt he was only a number. Bob worked better on a one-to-one basis. And so the Hendricks suggested that he join Christian Service Brigade. Here he had opportunity to participate and express himself within a small group of boys.

The Brigade provided summer-long camping programs, and Bob determined during those summer camping days that he wanted to have a camping ministry for the Lord. He plans to enter Dallas Theological Seminary to prepare himself for such a ministry. "All that's really involved in this," says Jeanne, "is getting to know your children well, taking the time to sense and meet their needs."

Knowing a child well, a parent senses when to let a child make his own decisions and when to step in. When Bev was between her sophomore and junior years at Wheaton College, she decided to take a quarter out and go to a secular school in Texas. She had it all fixed in her mind that she was going to live with two other girls in an apartment. Mother and daughter talked about it and Jeanne observed that for this daughter the situation would not be workable.

They talked about it at length, but Jeanne couldn't convince her daughter of the problems involved. Finally she determined that this move was definitely wrong and potentially harmful. She put her foot down.

"No, Bev, I cannot allow this!" said Jeanne.

"But Mother, I'm almost twenty years old. I can do what I want," replied Bev.

"No," reiterated Jeanne.

There were tears. But finally out of respect for her mother, Bev accommodated herself to her mother's decision. Sometime later, Bev was mature enough to come to her and say, "Mom, I'm so glad you made me do that. I can see the wisdom of it now."

"There are times," says Jeanne, "that a mother or father must use his prerogative as a parent and knowledge of the child to do what's best. In this case I just knew that Bev's personality was such that it wouldn't be a good situation for her."

When it comes to a parent's exercising authority, particularly in the teen years, Mrs. Hendricks has friends who have told her, "I'm afraid to exercise authority for fear I will lose my child."

"This fear stems from a lack of understanding of the child, what they are trying to do, and what they really want.

"One characteristic of the teen years, particularly middle and late adolescence, is that they are fighting for independence. In doing this they often make great and pompous statements about what they are going to do. In speaking so, they are pitting themselves against the authority of the parent."

Many parents fail to see the need for independence that the young person is trying to establish. And they also fail to see that the youth is hoping that parents will challenge him, because he is insecure about trying anything so adult on his own.

It's like an eleven-year-old insisting on driving the family car. He wants you to know he is grown up now and thinking about these things, but he is secretly hoping that you won't let him. He rightly suspects he cannot handle the car.

It may also be true of a daughter who insists on being able to wear immodest clothing. The parents must see that her challenge is a challenge for independence, and not always for the fashion as such. They should say no despite demands. For if they capitulate to the fear of losing her, and allow her to be indiscreet in her dress, the results can be disastrous.

"I contend from my experience that a parent who stands up to the child and challenges him—who says in a firm, but loving way, 'You're not going to do this!' or 'Why are you going to do this?'—will get much farther with the child and establish a mutual respect."

In helping a child find stable independence, a parent is wise to let the youth set most of his own limits. If a parent sets all the limits, this encourages the child to rebel for the sake of proving his independence. But allowing the child to set his own limits brings out a self-interest in the youth— because he realizes he must watch out for himself.

"I have found," says Jeanne, "that all of our children have set stricter limits for themselves than we have." Curfew was presented to the Hendricks kids as "Well, Barbara, what time do you feel you should get home tonight?"

"After our children had set their limits, we reminded them that that was the time we expected them." They were to call if something came up causing them to be delayed. Only once in all the children's teen-age years did one of the children arrive home past his own set curfew. And for this offense his car keys were taken away for two weeks.

"The real goal of a parent is not to bring a child from dependence to independence, but from dependence on the parents to dependence on the Lord." For this reason parental authority was deemphasized at the Hendricks home. God's authority was emphasized. The court of final appeal was ultimately not the parent, but the Lord and his Word.

"This is the surest possible way to garrison your children for a successful future."

The most important thing is that the child be given more and more freedom to make his own choices, emphasizing at the same time that now a higher authority will be lovingly directing him.

Third, in dealing with teen-agers, Jeanne recommends that a parent be quick to hear, slow to speak, slow to anger. "In every child there is a desire for parental approval. He wants to prove himself an adult just like Mom and Dad—and will do so, given half a chance.

"A big part of letting them become responsible adults is to listen to all their new ideas, inner feelings, and personal struggles. But what often happens is that the child is reluctant to come to Mom and Dad for sharing or advice. This usually happens because a parent has previously severed communications."

Communication may have been cut off by embarrassing a child in front of his peers. "Most disciplining should be done in private. Making your child look foolish in the eyes of his or her friends, particularly as a teen-ager, is a sure way to damage their faith in you."

Also, communication may be severed when a parent reacts hostilely to a child's unpredictable adolescent behavior. "Adolescents are often awkward and frustrated, and bound to make fools of themselves. A parent should guard against angry or degrading remarks such as 'Don't be so stupid!' or 'Get out of my sight!' "

Again, communication may be severed when a parent is not available when the child needs to talk. "It may be one A.M. when your teen-ager needs to get something off his chest, but whenever it is, take the time to *listen* to that child."

And last, communication can be hurt if a parent fails to take an interest in the details of a child's life. "If your son is interested in sports, then read up on sports, ask questions, and have a decent conversation with him. If your daughter wants to tell you about her friends, listen with interest and follow up about how they're doing.

"I have found that if I involve myself with my children's little world of nonessential topics, the children are assured that I'm interested. This pays off in big dividends. When they hit deep water or big questions that are really critical, they're going to come to me with that, too, because they've developed a habit of confiding in an understanding mom."

And when they ask serious questions that seem silly, or make statements that are seemingly outlandish, don't laugh at them. Take them seriously with, "Well, son, that's an idea to think about," or "That's an interesting question. Let's think about it."

In talking with their children, parents may need to set aside a special time as Howard and Jeanne do. Years ago they covenanted together to spend one hour a week with each child separately, where they would do whatever the child dictated. "The most effective communication that I have ever had with my children," says Howard Hendricks, "was in those hours."

"And also," says Jeanne, "we have to guard against being too narrow as Christians. For this reason, I try to read widely in magazines and books to keep abreast of what's happening. In addition, I've held down several jobs which have given me business experience and something from the outside to share. I know that some Christians would say a mother should *never* work, but in our situation it's been a necessity several times."

In regard to working and children, Jeanne says, "If you handle it right, with the idea that it's under God's leadership, that he ordered it right now, and that it's a temporary situation, the children will understand that you aren't trying to get away from them. And, as with any decision that is prompted by the Holy Spirit, it can prove profitable. Our children may even have come to greater maturity, as they were required to take on extra household chores and be more responsible for the sake of the family during these times."

A fourth rule for rearing teen-agers is to allow the child the luxury of a few mistakes. "In our household we have six independent people with such strong opinions on everything that we often bump heads and disagree. When they were younger, we would exercise full authority. But now that the children are older we take the tack that, if they bluntly disagree, we usually say, all right—but with a reminder that we don't agree with their decisions."

One time Bob went on a trip while he was away at college. Mom wrote a letter telling him she frankly disagreed with his decision, which upset Bob at the time. Later he confided to his dad that he probably made the wrong move. "But," says Jeanne, "I never said, 'I told you so,' and I didn't hold it against him. If a year later you're still throwing mistakes up to a child, it's bound to damage the parent-child relationship."

Once a parent-child decision has been arrived at, it's important that mom and dad stand with the youth in the decision. "When our first daughter decided to go to a certain college, we let her make the decision, just as we let all our children make their own decisions about higher education. 'We will be glad to give you any advice,' we said, 'but you have to live with that decision for the next four years.' " Barb chose a secular college but had a difficult time trying to cope with the pressures of secular campus life. She walked a spiritual tightrope for a while.

"Now we can go back and question that decision, but I personally feel that it was the right decision to make. Barb obviously needed to learn a few things. That's why, when God gives you peace about a decision, don't question it. It may get rough sometimes but that's all part of the process. And most of all, let your children know that you're standing with them in the decision, and that you'll see them through whatever their problems.

A fifth rule for rearing teen-agers is that parents should prepare their child ahead of time. "Good preparation is one of the best ways to give your child confidence, whether it is academic training where you spend extra time helping the slow reader in the family; spiritual training where you try to give them God's perspective on a situation to help orient them; social training, etc.

"If you are going to a wedding, and it's a first for your child, it's a good idea to let the son or daughter know just what is expected. Explain how to introduce yourself in a reception line, and give an idea of the traditional events so they will be aware of what's happening and why."

Jeanne remembers hearing her husband say many times to their boys, "So-and-so is coming over and I want you to get that hand out and give him a firm handshake. Say, 'How do you do? I'm Bill Hendricks, I'm glad to meet you.' "

"It's amazing how much confidence that gives a little kid, when he knows what to do in a situation." In addition to that, Jeanne comments that a hand on his shoulder (a little vote of confidence) often does wonders for a child.

A sixth rule for rearing teen-agers is that a parent should respect a young person's right to privacy. "I've always felt that it just wasn't fair to my children to misrepresent them to others. When my children fail in some way it's degrading to them to spread the news around. In the same way, when the children succeed I don't like to brag too much either because it inevitably puts pressure on them."

The Hendricks do give their children plenty of applause at home, however, encouraging them, but also reminding them that their talent and abilities are from the Lord. Bill was a successful star in his school play, *The Sound of Music.* It was a great triumph for him and brought him much praise and publicity.

On that occasion, Jeanne said, "Bill, I just want you to know that I'm very proud of you. You have tremendous talent and potential. But I want you to remember one thing—that everything you have, God has given to you. This puts a great responsibility on you, Bill, as to how you will use these gifts."

However a child performs, a parent should practice discretion in sharing information with others. This is paramount if they want their child's confidence. For the teen-ager must be sure that conquests or defeats are safe with Mom and Dad who can clearly interpret and appreciate the whole spectrum of the situation.

A seventh rule for rearing teen-agers is that parents should respond to their child in a nonthreatened way.

A child comes home from school announcing that the head cheerleader is pregnant, or that one of their classmates has been arrested for drugs. "At times like this, it's important that a parent react in a cool, somewhat detached way. If a parent reacts with too much anxiety to the news, it becomes an intriguing thing—to be further explored. This does not mean that a parent should skim over an issue such as drugs or immorality, but neither should it be given an excessive emotional response.

"When these things happen, a parent should see it as an opportunity." Barb's announcement about a pregnant cheerleader was made at the dinner table among the younger children, and the parents endeavored to ease the conversation away from the subject. Later, when Jeanne went to Barb's room, she brought up the subject again and used it as an opening to explain how such things as unwanted pregnancies could occur. "It's most important that when emotionally charged statements arise that parents neither exaggerate explanations nor go mute nor be embarrassed or shocked or overcome with fear. And the reason I can personally keep calm is that I have given each of my children to the Lord, and I believe that they are in his hands for safekeeping. Further, I can depend on him for rational and wise answers, and for subtle ways of handling difficult situations."

The eighth rule for rearing teen-agers is to watch for clues. During late adolescence their son went through what Jeanne called a "blackout" period. He was unenthusiastic, moody, depressed. He communicated in monosyllables.

"This was one of the most traumatic times of my life," says Jeanne. "He was so far from the Lord and from us. I felt like the devil himself was out to get my child. I prayed as I never had before."

It lasted for months, and finally came to a head when Howie and Jeanne went with their son to talk with his teacher about a grade he had changed on his report card.

After the confrontation at school, parents and son drove home together. On the way home the walls seemed to crumble. As they emerged from the car, the sixteen-year-old, in tears, put his arms around his mother. "Mom, I just don't understand why you still love me." As the communication reopened that night, Howie and Jeanne encouraged him to talk about his problems. Then they urged him to get things straight with the Lord. "We wanted to reassure him that we weren't condemning him as a person. 'This can happen to anybody,' we said, 'and we'll help you in any way we can to get these problems worked out.'"

So the spiritual area was straightened out. Then the Hendricks helped their son get other areas untangled.

"The whole point of this illustration, is that when the child is going through situations, watch for the hints he gives you of trouble in his life."

Of course, this is why parents should give much time to their children. "Some mothers spend much time in household details. Often a clean home is more important to them than a happy child." Howard Hendricks comments that as a child he lived in an immaculately kept house, but with some problem relationships.

"I rise up and call my wife blessed every chance I get," he said, "because she taught me that a child's feelings are more important than fastidious housekeeping."

A tenth rule for rearing teen-agers is to *believe God for your child.* "A woman who fully commits her life and her child's life to God has prayer authority. When I faced the battle with Satan over my son, I talked forcefully with God. I reminded him that this boy was committed to him, and that I expected him to bring my son out of this dilemma."

There have been other big decisions for which Jeanne has had to exercise her faith. "It has been our practice to get the kids out of the nest as soon as possible, and so at an early age the children went to week-long camps and then to summer-long camps. Finally we encouraged them to take summer jobs."

At sixteen, Barbara left for Schroon Lake, New York, to counsel at a Christian camp for the summer. "I believed with all my heart that this step was important for Barbara. I wanted her to be semi-independent by the time she entered college so that she wouldn't flounder as so many young people do."

But at the same time it was a difficult decision for Jeanne to let her daughter make this trip by herself. While she was there, Barbara became ill. "This is a situation where I felt I was being tested and trained just as much as Barbara was," Jeanne confided. "I had to place my faith for my child's safety in God."

Another time Bev was injured in an auto accident and was rushed to Baylor Hospital. Jeanne remembers the phone call, asking her to go to the emergency room. On the way down she said, "Lord, I've asked you to prepare me for something like this. My husband is in California, and I may have to make decisions tonight that involve thousands of dollars or long-term therapy. Lord, I've got to have my wits about me, I've got to know what I'm doing. And I've got to act like a responsible adult. It's up to you to help me do it."

Jeanne walked into the hospital and saw a young girl's face covered with blood and with teeth out of place. In that situation Jeanne maintained such composure that it caused the doctor and some of the staff to comment later about her tranquility.

Another time their oldest daughter was engaged to a young man who her parents felt was not appropriate for her. It was a three-year relationship and words failed in advising their daughter. Finally the Hendricks, together, covenanted with God to leave the predicament squarely in his hands. "It was only a week later that our daughter broke her relationship with this young man. It was a lesson to us again that we could believe God for our children. We really needn't worry about them if we have committed them to him.

"It's important in all the decisions you make with your children that you act on the relationship gone before. If they have respect for you, and your word carries great weight, then you may have more freedom to voice approval or disapproval. If the relationship is strained, it may be better to keep silent and practice loving them instead.

"I don't palm myself off as any super Christian, because I know myself too well. But I do know that to be a successful Christian mother you have to learn to seek God's wisdom on a regular basis.

"I have a healthy respect for the pressures of the world my children live in. I know what can happen to them. And I have no illusions about it—they're great kids, but they're made out of the same stuff I am. They can fall any time, any place. This makes me feel tremendously responsible. So I do my best to study the Word, because I believe it's the only true source of authority. John 6:63 has meant a great deal to me recently, 'The words that I speak to you—they are spirit and they are life.'

"And then, I take the Word of God and try to put common sense with it as far as advising my children. Yes, our children are turning out to honor the Lord. But believe me, we give God all the credit."

Four
Wanda Jones

As a minister's family the Joneses spent much of their time traveling from city to city with Dad on his preaching engagements. The oldest girls, two years apart, made an important discovery on these trips. Not only did they like to sing, but they *could* sing—and sing well! This wasn't surprising since both parents were musical. Wanda Jones sang and played the piano. Howard Jones, who is now a leading evangelist for the Billy Graham team, had been a saxophonist in a jazz band.

One afternoon in their Cleveland home Wanda made a few suggestions. The children were singing "Jesus Loves Me" and she asked her oldest daughter to try a second part. With her mother's help Cheryl learned her part by late afternoon.

"There's still another part. Gail, how about trying the alto?" suggested Wanda. It took more than an afternoon to work out Gail's part, but in one week "Jesus Loves Me" was sung in three parts.

When the girls were announced at their church Christmas program everyone clapped, but the audience wasn't prepared for what they were going to hear. The girls stood close together, knees shaking, hoping their parents would stay

---

Wanda Jones, mother of five, is active as a teacher of retarded children, and also as a singer and pianist. Her husband, Howard, is an evangelist with the Billy Graham Evangelistic Association. The Jones family lives in Oberlin, Ohio.

close by. Then Wanda sounded the chord and "Jesus the Light of the World" flowed out in full harmony. It electrified the listeners to hear three-year-old Phyllis, five-year-old Gail, and seven-year-old Cheryl glorifying the Lord in song.

Looking back Mrs. Jones recalls, "It's important to begin involving children early in a Christian ministry. Children must see where they are needed. If they find satisfaction and a place where they can contribute within Christian service, a parent needn't fear that they will change later on in life to a pursuit where Christ is not honored."

And so the girls began a musical ministry. Within a few years the family had moved to Monrovia, Liberia, to reside at radio station ELWA. Here the young singing trio had their own radio program called "Teen Time." Wanda wrote the scripts. The girls would read *Little Pilgrim's Progress* adapted for radio and including music.

With pats on the back and encouraging words from their parents, the trio could see how their lives were counting for Christ. While in Liberia and still teen-agers the girls sang at their first Billy Graham crusade. Later, invitations came from many parts of the world to sing for Jesus Christ. When they returned to the United States the girls put out their first record, and later produced other albums for a well-known record company. Over the years they have inspired many people in churches, at crusades, and on radio and TV in the United States and abroad.

David, the fourth child and only boy, also had gifts that he particularly wanted to develop for the Lord. When the family was in Liberia, he'd often observe his dad "passing the word." This was the phrase used for going out and sharing the gospel. David admired his dad. Perhaps this is what sparked him one Sunday afternoon to gather some of his own friends, leave the house with tracts and New Testament, and head for a neighboring village.

The people must have been astounded to see a seven-year-old boy rounding up the villagers to hear the gospel. When he returned home that afternoon he awakened his Daddy from siesta. "Daddy, Daddy, guess whàt I've been doing!"

And before his dad could answer, David exclaimed, "I've been out passing the word!" Cupped in his hands were collected pennies. He had followed his father's example even to taking up the offering.

Dad was perplexed. David had left the compound without permission from his parents. Not wanting to spoil his son's enthusiasm, Howard reminded him that it was important to get permission before entering a village to "pass the word." Also he cautioned David that it would please God for him to consult with his parents the next time he wanted to evangelize Liberia. But David wasn't discouraged. Immediately he asked his Dad to help him prepare a sermon. He was already planning his next venture.

One child-rearing observer has commented, "If they love you, they'll love your Jesus." Perhaps that is the reason why these children were so anxious to follow in the footsteps of their parents. The children looked up to their parents so much that they wanted to be like them.

One problem the Joneses helped their children with is the problem of being black in a basically white culture.

"Numerous times," Mr. Jones said, "I observed white children making fun of our children's color. It's difficult when it's done to you. But when it's done to your children it's almost unbearable. We have had to help our children gain self-respect and learn to handle the inevitable resentment."

One time when David had just started to school he returned home and asked, "Mother, what's wrong with my color?" A little bit shaken, Wanda discussed with David how God looks at races. "The true divisions in the Bible," she explained, "are not according to color or race—but spirituality. There are those who live for God and those who don't."

And then she referred David to Jesus himself. His was a hated race. He underwent much persecution. Yet Jesus didn't react with vengeance. John, one of his disciples, wanted to call down fire from heaven on the Samaritans for rejecting Jesus, but Jesus knew that the situation rested ultimately in God's hands. God himself would weigh things and bring about justice.

Then Wanda shared the story of Simon of Cyrene, the black man who was identified with the cross of Christ. "Just as he had to bear a cross," she explains to the children, "we may have to bear a cross too. But the important thing is that Christ is honored in our lives no matter what we go through."

Of course a big help in this situation was having Mom and Dad tell the children about their own similar encounters with racism in one form or another. They had felt painful rejection, but Christ gave them power to overcome it with love. This helped the child to see that they could weather the storm as well.

An added problem was to explain the negative reaction of some Christians to the color of David's skin. "It was one thing to explain to him how to react to an unbeliever's prejudices, but far more difficult to explain how a Christian could also be guilty of having race prejudice."

The girls' trio missed many invitations to sing simply because they were black. Some white Christian organizations did not believe in integration in the Lord's work and excluded the Joneses. But Dr. and Mrs. Jones would take the biblical perspective and relate it directly to the children's lives. "If you keep seeking the Lord's will, he will open closed doors. You should not take vengeance or hold resentment against anyone who mistreats or rejects you because of your race."

The Jones family has also had their share of persecution from some militant blacks. When one daughter was attending a Bible college, she went to a meeting where a few black male students talked about invading white churches by force. Their approach was not biblical and was in fact contrary to Christian principles. After one person suggested that they carry out their plan, the Joneses' daughter stood and said: "I don't feel that this is pleasing to God. It isn't showing Christian love in this situation. Violence is not the Christian answer. Love, not hate, must control us. I feel that under all circumstances we should maintain love and approach the problem in a Christian way." After she had said this, a black girl in front of her turned around, slapped her across the face, and knocked her to the floor.

"What did you do?" Mrs. Jones asked, when she heard what had happened. "I didn't think I should fight back," Gail replied. "I was stunned and hurt. But I knew I would have to leave the situation in God's hands. I prayed for the girl who struck me. I decided to follow yours and Dad's example and good advice and love back. Now I've learned what it means to suffer for righteousness' sake, and to bear it all for Christ." "That was right," Wanda answered. "God keeps an accurate score of what happens on earth. And if you keep living for him, without bitterness in your heart, there *will* be a great reward."

Of course this principle of trusting God is primary for any child of any color to understand. All parents somewhere along the line are going to see their child experience rejection from a peer group or a grown-up. Just as Mrs. Jones has done, this is a time to instill God's perspective in the child: that God is greater than all situations, circumstances, or people's opinions.

Very early a Christian child should learn the biblical perspective that he is "in Christ." A wise parent will look for situations to teach this truth and trust God to work it out in a way that will convince the child that he is secure in the love of Christ. It may be helpful for the mother to do some Bible study with him on what this means. "We aren't to get our identity from around us, but from the Word of God."

> Whoever touches you touches the apple of my eye (Zech. 2:8).
>
> You are as a sweet smelling savor to God (2 Cor. 2:15).
>
> I have loved you with an everlasting love (Jer. 31:3).
>
> I have called you by your own name. You are mine (Isa. 43:1).
>
> You are precious in my sight (Isa. 43:4).

According to many psychologists, the area of identity and self-image is the foundation of either failure or success in an individual. God's perspective of a Christian, the only true one, is a firm foundation.

One day Lisa came home from school and told her parents that she had been called an "oreo." This meant that she was black outside and white inside, a derogatory statement. She experienced conflicting emotions when some of her black friends told her that she should wear an afro to identify with her race. Here again the problem of identity came up.

Howard Jones wisely answered his daughter, "Identity is not typified by what you wear or how you do your hair, but by who you *are*. Your true identity is found in God who created you. You are a Christian. You reign as royalty on this earth. A Christian need never be an imitator," he told her. "You can allow God to keep you an individual. And," he added, "you are part of the race that God has made you. You can trust God to help you keep your dignity and self-respect in spite of what others may say against you."

Now four of her children have left home. The oldest, Cheryl, is married, David is in college, Phyllis is a stewardess for Delta Airlines, and Gail is soon to enroll in training school for United stewardesses. Lisa is at home, a high school freshman, and Mrs. Jones is getting ready for one of the best periods of her life.

"I admit that it was traumatic when I saw the children beginning to leave the nest. But the Lord has provided."

One of the times she was most aware of the change was at Christmas time several years ago. The whole family was back for Christmas. Twelve-year-old Lisa seemed to sense her mother's feelings. She observed how her mother tried to make the time slow down, how she referred to many happy moments when the children were all at home, and how she held back the tears at the end of the holidays. As the older children began to leave, Lisa came up to her mother and said, "Mother, you still have me! What would you do if I hadn't come along?" "Lisa," her mother said as though a bright light had pierced the fog, "you know that's true. God knew that I would be lonely and he gave you to me for this time." "I guess," says Wanda, "that this is just another reminder that for the woman who seeks to honor God, he'll meet her every need—whatever stage of her life it is!

"There's never any cause to feel that the years after the children leave home are going to be lonely or unchallenging." Even though statistics show that alcoholism in women is highest in the forty-to-fifty age range—which indicates that these years are difficult for many women—Mrs. Jones believes that women can be aided by keeping in mind a few principles.

First, prepare for the middle-age years. Mrs. Jones had some college and was able to take additional courses to prepare herself for the work she is now doing: helping retarded children. Also in her years of being a mother, she devoted time to Bible study. Now, with extra time, she is involved in teaching a weekly Bible study. And of course she has wonderful trips to look forward to and opportunities to minister with Howard.

In thinking through her life, a woman should begin early to ask the question, "What will I do when the children leave home?" And she should pray and seek God's wisdom for some kind of plan that will be fulfilling and useful. (This is obviously a word of wisdom to young single women who are so anxious to get married that they are willing to skip college or vocational training.)

Second, it's important that a mother gain a new perspective on herself. She will need to relinquish her authoritarian role as a mother and relate now as a friend and available guide to her children. This is difficult for many women. Perhaps it's because they haven't found their own purpose for these later years. A mother should be aware of feeling sorry for herself, or putting a burden on her children or husband to meet her needs—rather then depending on God to supply ingenuity and creativeness in finding her new role.

It seems that many women today want to get out into a ministry or vocation before their children are grown. "But the home is good preparation soil for a later prosperous ministry." And since Wanda has not escaped the challenge of the home she has much to offer, particularly to younger women.

The Scripture gives a direct command on this subject, "Older women are to instruct the young women" (Tit. 2:4).

"There are so many needs among young girls, particularly those from non-Christian homes. They need counsel and guidance in their single days, in their early married life, and with their children. And now I have a time when I can offer understanding and advice to many young women who need this help."

Third, a woman should remember her importance during these later years. "Be careful not to follow society's norms of early retirement, which can shelve people long before God's intended time. There are great opportunities and it's the older person who often has the wisdom and experience to do the most good. Surely when a person's usefulness is over, God will take her home. Until that time it's important that she seek and keep strong faith in God to utilize her abilities and learning in the later years.

"I don't want to minimize the problems here; it's a shaky time. But we have a stable God. If we have continued in a walk with the Lord over the years, there will be no need to panic as we take still another step of faith."

One verse that has sustained Mrs. Jones for many years is 2 Corinthians 9:8—"And God is able to make all grace and favor abound toward you; that you'll always have complete sufficiency in everything, so that you may be able to do every good work." For a mother at any stage in her life this verse is assurance that "God can meet every single need."

Five
Kathleen Santucci

Upon receiving a tape about this book and a list of questions, Mrs. Hugo Santucci wanted to draw out the opinions and memories of her three daughters still at home. They first talked about creating a desire for wisdom in a child. What things make him or her reach for understanding in the highest kind of Christian living?

Immediately one of her girls mentioned that parents inevitably communicated to their children what is important to them. If it's important to the parent to be wise, it will be important to the children to be wise. Christian values and goals that the parents have—not the ones that they think they should have, but what their children actually see lived out—set the standard for the children.

One of the girls mentioned that since reading was an important part of the Santucci family, this automatically communicated that learning was an important part of their lives. Another said, "Well, knowledge is not the same as wisdom." Claire mentioned that reading the book of Proverbs and

---

Kathleen Santucci received a B. A. degree in Psychology from the University of California. She has been active in Women's Bible Study Fellowship, and now regularly teaches the Bible to about forty women. Her husband, Hugo, is professor of Bible at the California Center of Biblical Studies. The Santuccis have five children and live in Culver City, California.

memorizing certain verses in the Proverbs as a family had tremendous effect on her desire to reach out for true Christian wisdom.

The girls said that a significant factor in developing wisdom came from their parents' having other people in their home. "People of all different kinds became integral parts of our lives," Kathleen remarked, "and the openness with which we shared our lives with each of them communicated to our four girls, and later on to our son, Peter, the contrast between their lives and our lives. Many people came to share their problems with us. After they would leave, I would discuss, on an appropriate level, the problems these people had and how they had become involved in them. I believe this gave our children a lot of understanding about what makes life tick."

One of the girls mentioned that her mother listened to them discuss their own problems and endeavored to work through solutions with them. This was an important part in their developing wisdom about life. "In recent years, as our older girls are beginning to leave home, I find that on the whole they have good judgment. I personally link this to the amount of wisdom and good thinking we have tried to instill in them over the years."

The Santucci girls and their mother then shifted to the subject of humor. The first thing the girls said was that they considered having a sense of humor crucial for the problems of life. Difficult tensions in the family were resolved only when they learned together to develop a sense of humor and find the funniness in things that weren't funny. They describe this as the best escape valve and release from tension that a person can have.

The girls also felt that this was an important part of being a flexible person: that anger could be released through humor. In many situations of life you can do only one of two things, laugh or cry. This reminded Kathleen of when she was in Athens last summer. She had turned around one of those little revolving displays of post cards, something the owner of the art store apparently never anticipated anybody would do. It caught the corner of one of his oil paintings, which flipped forward, and then it was like ten-pins on a bowling alley. Each picture as it went forward caught the picture ahead of it until the entire display in the store went flat on its face. "This was far from funny, but it really made us laugh."

The girls made another point. A sense of humor must always be sensitive to others. This reminded Kathleen of a predawn episode in the Israeli airport at Tel Aviv. Unknown to her, a hijacking was going on that involved Israel. Security regulations required that every single item was to be taken out of suitcases. The woman ahead of Mrs. Santucci was very upset at being treated in this manner.

"We tried to make light of the situation for her with humor. But the young Israeli woman who was examining the contents of our suitcases was very tense. She finally flared out at me for treating the whole situation so lightly. I tried to explain to her that the woman ahead of me was of a sensitive racial group and felt discriminated against. I was trying to ease her situation. It was a good example of how very sensitive you have to be in the use of humor." The girls added that if the person with you isn't mature enough to see the humor in the situation then you will just have to laugh in your heart.

Taking things lightly or taking things seriously may require subtle wisdom. For example, when six-year-old Peter came in with a wood peg in his mouth, smoking it like a cigar, this was something Kathleen reacted to lightly. "To react seriously would have been a mistake," she said. "It would seem that you were really afraid he might do something like this. To react in humor suggests that it is so incongruous with what you expect of him that there is no way to take it except lightly and humorously."

Yet at times children don't want to be taken lightly. They want to be dead serious. Nothing offends them more at such a time than a parent's refusal to take them seriously. This is one reason why a parent's antennae have to be out all the time toward their children. Children want to be taken seriously as worthy persons. But they hope that their mistakes and their trial periods will be taken a little bit lightly. If they are not repeated patterns that really need to have some talking through and working out, then a little lightness is valuable.

"Also there are so many things a child, a teen-ager, even an adult tests out. They have to be given the right to test things through, to try them. Initially I think a parent ought to take a light view in order to give that child this privilege. This is really difficult with the first child and much easier with the following children."

Another question that stimulated conversation between Mrs. Santucci and her children was habit training. The biggest influence on Kathleen in this area was Dr. Rudolf Dreikurs from the University of Chicago, author of *Challenge of Parenthood* and *Children to Challenge.* He strongly emphasized the idea that every act has a consequence. The most damaging thing a parent can do is to interfere with the natural consequences of their children's actions. If their actions are wrong, then the consequences should become their deterrent. His only exception to this was if the child's health or life was in jeopardy.

"We are in agreement at our home that good habits and good patterns are not to be rewarded with money or bribes of any sort, but with praise, acceptance, and approval. The matter of praise in developing proper habits is something that I have never done as much of as I wish I had," she adds, "and that I can't encourage enough in any parent." Mrs. Santucci will never forget a little boy about three years old. He was swimming and his father was praising every move he made. This boy strove and strove harder to swim for the approval of his father. "Parental approval is something that every child seeks as a normal feeling. As a parent I have never quite utilized its full power.

"Withdrawal of approval is so serious that parents should save it only for extreme situations. Otherwise they should be lavish in the approval they give for every commendable thing. This should not be handled in a phony way, but in a sense of genuine appreciation. It isn't necessarily how much they say, but it's the attitude, the genuine enthusiasm and realness with which they say it."

Claire reminded her mother about her last music teacher in high school. One of her great features was that though she found things to criticize in the pieces that Claire played, she never failed also to find good.

One of the hardest things to realize is how many habits are trained into a child in the first part of life. Dr. Dreikurs emphasized that what won't be accepted in an older child is not to be accepted in an infant or small child. Parental attitude should be consistent from the beginning. When such consistency is practiced all along, it makes for a predictable situation for a child. And this is considered most important by every professional in the child guidance field.

Some bad habits are simply reactions against parents. Messy rooms seem to be a particularly obvious expression of hidden conflict with parents. The point then is not to deal with the bad habit symptom, but to find out where the underlying conflict between the parent and child is. When that is resolved the bad habit clears up, but the process may be a slow one.

The biggest problem with training in good habits is doing it with fun, good will, and consistency when children are young. Every year into the teens, the parent has less time to develop that particular human personality and train it in proper habits.

Mrs. Santucci's oldest daughter observed that while she was in high school she didn't have one school friend whose family operated together as a family unit. She considered the most significant of her own family's patterns to be attending church together Sunday morning, followed by a special family dinner. She could count on the best family dinner of the week to follow the time at church, and this added appeal to church attendance. It strongly unified the family one day out of the week.

If any of the children became restless with Sunday pattern of living, Hugo and Kathleen tried to loosen the pattern a little. They encouraged them to bring somebody into the home rather than going out of the home: somebody with a compatible viewpoint and religious outlook on life. On some occasions the children were involved in party celebrations or visits to Disneyland on Sunday. Usually they found that being together with the family on Sunday had become so important to them that they lost more by going than they gained.

Something that was remembered as very special was the pattern of their father's making fresh biscuits for Sunday tea just before they went to church in the evening. To have tea together was very simple, but it had the feel of a special family tradition.

Another thing that tended to amplify the pleasure of Sunday and church going was that from time to time they stopped at an ice cream parlor after church on a Sunday evening. This was something the Santuccis did on only two other occasions: after the girls had participated in either a graduation or a piano recital. So it was associated with something significant. In short, Sunday was such a special day that nobody wanted to be left out.

There were other family patterns that the girls remembered well. One of the best loved things the family did together, maybe once a year, was to have a picnic in Golden Gate Park in San Francisco. This was more often than not on a Sunday after church, with everything loaded in the car before they left for church.

Then there was the selection of the Christmas tree. For the Santucci family this meant a trip to one of the tree farms in the area, which involved all sorts of rain and slush. One time the car even got torn out underneath, but it always added to their Christmas celebration. Going together out into the woods was part of establishing family unity.

At this point one of the girls picked up on this idea. "Family unity helped me learn the value of nonconformity. The strength of being part of the family group helped to give me the courage to resist patterns outside the home that were undesirable." From earliest years the children were taught that somebody else's doing something doesn't make it right.

In order to do what was right, one had to be free not to have to conform. This is where family unity paid off.

Another topic Kathleen and the girls tossed around was, "How does a parent help a teen-ager through teen-age romances?" "I don't know much about this matter of traumatic crushes," Kathleen said. "I think I have had fewer problems than some others. Our children know that I consider in-depth early and midteen-age romantic involvements as an interference with the full development of their personalities and abilities.

"I taught our girls not even to date a boy who didn't have personal faith in God and serious concern for God's direction of his life. Generally I have been very thankful for the girls' response and am sure they have avoided some undesirable situations and problems. And the temporary defaults from this pattern only served to be convincing of the value of the rule.

"I, myself, am convinced that the area of boy-girl relations is definitely not a subject about which a mother should be romantic or sentimental. Then of all times she needs to have her feet on the ground. Periodically, when my daughters are in an open, talking frame of mind, I can point out exactly where they stand in their relations with boys. I find that girls inevitably are afraid of their parents in a situation like this. No matter how much love you've demonstrated, even if you could be 100 percent perfect, they would still be afraid that somehow or other you are going to interfere with all the beautiful things that lie ahead of them in this great romantic world. At such a time as this I would try to have a conversation in which I showed great concern for them but also strongly laid out the situation to help them see the way they were acting and where it was leading them. I would ask the question, 'Is this what you really want?' I would then try to help them ascertain what it was they really wanted out of life —not what I wanted for them—but what *they* really wanted. Was this relationship going to interfere with their maintaining this important goal or help them in attaining it?

"One daughter once went into the blues over a broken

relationship. We assessed the situation over and over again. I kept pressing on her the importance of not allowing herself to be turned inward and nourish her unhappiness but to start reaching out to others. She told me much later that she had really hated me when I had told her these things, but that it had actually helped her. At the time of discussion she had said that her friends really felt sorry for her. I said, 'That's what friends are for—to feel sorry for you—but parents are to help you see yourself, to help you come to grips with the situation and mature as much as possible.' "

This California mother of five commented on the difficulty her girls found in understanding how sensitive to sexual arousal young men are. "So periodically we hash it all over again, preferably with Hugo around to reinforce that this is not just a woman's imagination. I've always taught them that their actions are forms of communication. If they use up all their actions of love with somebody who has little meaning to them, then they will have nothing left with which to create the really meaningful message to the special person. I've told them what it meant to me, at the time that I responded to my husband's proposal of marriage, to have the keen delight of having a pure gift in myself to give to him. This is something that I had never anticipated. I don't even remember being told about it, but the realization of it was a quiet ecstasy. This is putting the issue on a positive level for the girls."

The girls and their mother next discussed how to keep a child from being involved with the wrong crowd. Linda's immediate reaction was, "You just don't get *involved* in a wrong crowd because you go by your parents' values."

"Yet," added Kathleen, "I occasionally saw exceptions, and this was a time to spend money on providing an adventuresome form of Christian service far enough away from home. Hugo and I spend our money carefully, but Christian ventures for our children which stimulate and direct them into serious commitment to Christ have always been a financial priority. Nevertheless the decision to go off somewhere had to be at our children's initiative, not at our suggestions and prodding. Our oldest daughter, full of the adventure of life, met her husband on a Christian service mission in France."

Asked about adolescent emotions, Kathleen expressed positive feelings about them. "The coming alive of emotions enables youth to have a coming-alive response to the call of Jesus Christ as a living person. I find the whole awakening of adolescent emotions a dynamic opportunity. So when they're distressed about them, I try to explain the potential that these new emotions have to offer them. This helps them have a different viewpoint, even though the going is rough.

"As a mother I have gradually learned to encourage free expression. It's quite natural for this to be easier for the mother than for the father, because he is sensitive to his position as head of the home and spends much less time with the children. In recent years, since Hugo left business for Christian service, he's been more accessible and encourages expression as much as I do. I find everything to be gained by letting children divulge their thinking and nothing to lose."

Kathleen was candid about how long she has been in learning the concept and understanding its value. She appreciates Paul Tournier's book, *The Strong and the Weak,* which helped her understand why she had formerly avoided confrontation and then the importance of confrontation of the right kind. "I learn so much from my children just by listening to them. We all have blind spots about ourselves and need another family member's perspective."

Recently Linda and Claire had been building up an "out of sorts" feeling with each other for the first time since they'd been sharing a room together. In talking to each one separately Kathleen came to the conclusion that some sort of confrontation was needed. Neither of the girls desired it, so the confrontation came about at Mom's prodding. They brought out painful irritations. Kathleen pressed them on which ones they wanted her help with. The result was that each one yielded up some "rights" to space and convenience that made living together more tolerable for the other. "This openness of expression has proved itself over and over again to be valuable."

Both Claire and Linda had already, in their understanding of the tension between themselves, looked for what they felt was the root reason behind the irritations. "I think the whole family is accustomed to looking beneath the surface for the real irritation and the real problem. We are used to assessing people and situations on a regular basis without trying to eliminate the negative in the assessing. We look at people as people, as though they have a right to fail, a right to hurt themselves. Yet we stress that we suffer the consequences of our actions.

"As the children mature I think more expression is in order. I'm sure that if children past high school age aren't treated as cooperating adults they will find some way to leave home. I think that today the appeal of relationship is not nearly so much on the basis of parental authority as on profound respect. I think a big part of the reason our children respect us is that we give them the right to be themselves and express themselves. But you must understand that in doing this we are seeing them as made in the image of God, so that being themselves is their unique expression of this image.

"I think primarily I look on all the girls as adults even though Joy is only fifteen and Linda seventeen. I look on our family as an adult Christian community in which my job is to help them wherever they want my help. I try to maintain an orderly environment in which we can function as smoothly as possible and a spiritual environment in which we live in warm responsiveness together."

Finally, Claire commented to her mother about something that had helped her mature into an independent person. Kathleen wrote Claire a letter when she was eighteen. In it was sketched a word picture of the new life her daughter would be entering. She would be drawing on human resources of good judgment and wisdom that had been carefully developed by discerning parents. She would be counting on the divine resources of God and Christ. Life's hurdles were ahead of her, presenting challenge as well as a responsibility. It was a turning point in helping her accept her new role as an adult.

But this wasn't the end of Kathleen's role of motherhood in Claire's life either. Always her goal would be to be there when her daughter needed her, to communicate confidence that she could and would make it to her own goals. The bond of love Claire and the other Santucci children have with their parents is eternal because its foundation is in God himself.

Six
Vonette Bright

"It used to be that parents would worry if their children weren't popular. Now they worry if they are." Vonette Bright, wife of Bill Bright, founder and director of Campus Crusade for Christ, expressed this thought at a women's luncheon. Then she continued, "With the particular demands and stresses that children experience today, it is more important than ever that parents be men and women whom God can use to affect their children's lives."

Some time ago at a luncheon in San Diego, Mrs. Bright met a discouraged woman who told about her son. It seems that the boy was stealing car tires and throwing them into the ocean just to erase his boredom. The distraught mother would often say, "Son, if you would only get into the church and find a new set of friends, you could pick up new habits and you wouldn't be doing these things." The mother persisted and coaxed until one day the irritated son spoke up. "Mom," he said, "why do you keep telling me about the church? I can't see that it's ever done you any good."

After relating this story, the mother told Vonette that she wasn't sure she knew the God whom Vonette knew. "The

---

Vonette Bright currently heads the Great Commission Prayer Crusade. Her husband, Bill, is founder and director of Campus Crusade for Christ. They have two sons and live in San Bernardino, California, the home of CCC international headquarters.

more I try to be a Christian," she said, "the more uptight I get. It seems the harder I try, the more impossible it is." So Vonette described her own experience.

"I grew up in the church. I was active in youth training services. I made sure every time the church door was open, I was there. And yet, as I entered college, it seemed that God meant less and less to me."

After her faith had been bombarded by endless questions she finally decided that Christianity was designed to make people behave themselves. She further concluded that there wasn't any reality of God in a person's life. "If there was, I was sure that by this time I would have known it," she told herself.

And yet Vonette was willing to weigh her morals with anyone. She looked upon herself as a good person and decided that if anybody would make it to heaven she would.

"It was at this time that a man named Bill Bright entered my life. As our relationship grew and as our marriage seemed imminent, Bill's newly found faith in Christ was beginning to bother me. He was so zealous that he planned to enter seminary." In his letters Vonette would often find requests for prayer and she thought to herself, "A person needs to be far more devout than I am to get answers from God." Bill would also send back Bible passages for her to think about. "It became more and more obvious that we were headed in different directions."

At this point Vonette made up her mind that she would have to save Bill from his fanaticism. In the meantime he had asked her to attend a conference with him in California. It was here that she had a great surprise. "All about me were students and young people, doctors, lawyers, actors and actresses, and they all had something different about their lives. They had an obvious purpose for living. They had a certain happiness that I had never seen before."

The students would say to Vonette, "Have you heard the answer to prayer God gave me?" Or, "Listen to what I learned in the Bible today." Vonette concluded from this that the religious zeal she was observing was merely the product of "new Christians." She had grown up in the church. It wasn't new to her. She just thought that their zeal would die down once they got more settled with being a Christian.

But still Vonette realized that she and Bill didn't have the same goals in mind for their life. His goal was to serve God fully with his whole heart. And Vonette was unable to make a similar commitment. Finally she reached the conclusion that she would never understand the Christian life as Bill understood it. She decided to break off their engagement. But then Bill suggested that she talk with Dr. Henrietta Mears, director of Christian Education at First Presbyterian Church of Hollywood.

A former chemistry professor, Miss Mears was aware of the intellectual problems that faced Vonette. After some time Miss Mears suggested that the problem between God and man was not primarily intellectual. "The true problem is sin!"

Of course this didn't strike Vonette Zachary well. She insisted on her own goodness until Miss Mears pointed out that the definition of sin in the Bible simply means "to miss the mark."

"It doesn't have to mean that you have committed gross or immoral acts, Vonette," she said. "It may involve a lack of love or discipline, failure to believe God, or pride." And suddenly Vonette got the point. She hadn't fully measured up to the standards that God had set.

"The work that God did on the cross," Miss Mears continued, "was to take the punishment for all your failure to measure up to God's standards. When the Bible says to believe in Christ, it means to know that he is your *personal* Savior from sin."

At this point Vonette made the decision to ask Jesus Christ to be her personal Savior. Now her attitude changed. She didn't have all the answers to the Christian faith, but she now agreed with Bill that every person should know Christ personally.

"It's not so important that you know when you became a

Christian or what the circumstances were," Vonette comments today. "What will make the biggest difference is that you know for sure that you have received him. You are his child. Heaven is your destiny. And such assurance of Christ in your life is an absolute necessity if you are to grow in your Christian faith."

Perhaps Vonette's background of not clearly realizing until her college years how a person comes to Christ has made her even more determined to see that her children attain "new life" in Christ at the earliest age possible. As to what age to share the gospel with a child, one good rule would be that as soon as a child recognizes that he has sinned, he can usually understand his need for a Savior.

One effective tool for sharing the message of Christ to a child is the "Good News Comic Book" published by Campus Crusade for Christ. It is reprinted here for the use of the reader.

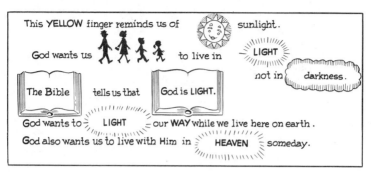

This **YELLOW** finger reminds us of sunlight.

God wants us to live in

The Bible tells us that God is LIGHT.

God wants to LIGHT our WAY while we live here on earth.

God also wants us to live with Him in HEAVEN someday.

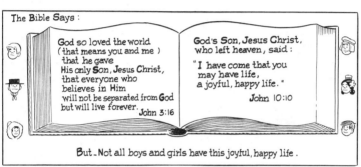

The Bible Says:

God so loved the world (that means you and me) that he gave His only Son, Jesus Christ, that everyone who believes in Him will not be separated from God but will live forever. John 3:16

God's Son, Jesus Christ, who left heaven, said:

"I have come that you may have life, a joyful, happy life."

John 10:10

But — Not all boys and girls have this joyful, happy life.

This **DARK** finger tells why. It says:

All men, women, boys, and girls are sinful and separated from God.

This is why they cannot know and enjoy God's **LOVE** and **PLAN** for their lives.

For all have sinned and have not lived up to the perfect goodness of God.

Romans 3:23

WHAT IS SIN?

Sin is not knowing God; not caring about God.. Wanting to have **OUR WAY**, not **GOD'S WAY**.

Have you ever been unkind? Told a lie? Been angry? Disobeyed your parents? Stolen anything? Hated anybody? Cheated?

People do these things because they are separated from God.

This **DARK** finger tells us that all have sinned.

GOD is **LIGHT** as the **YELLOW** finger tells us.

But we are going our **WAY** in the **DARKNESS** of **SIN**

Sin separates us from God and God's Way.

> For the wages of sin is death (spiritual separation from God).
> Romans 6:23

This is <u>not</u> GOOD NEWS, is it?
And I told you that this was a GOOD NEWS GLOVE.

This **RED** finger tells us:

> God shows His love for us.
> While we were still sinners,
> Jesus Christ died for us.
> We have been saved from the
> punishment of sin by the blood of Christ.
>
> Romans 5:8-9

That means that He was punished for our sins.
HE took our place.

At **CHRISTMAS** we celebrate the birth of Jesus.

Heaven Jesus

John 1:14
God became man.

His name shall be Jesus
For He shall save His
people from their
sins.
Matthew 1:21

At **Easter** we remember that...

He died

was buried

and came alive again;
1 Corinthians 15:3-4
Jesus Christ lives forever.

This is why Jesus Christ can say:

> I am the **WAY**
> the **TRUTH**
> the **LIFE**
> No man woman boy or girl
> can come to God, the heavenly Father,
> but by me.   John 14:6

GOD

Jesus

SIN

This is **GOOD NEWS** !

But : It is not enough just to know these **3** things .

God loves me .
I have sinned .
Jesus died and came alive for me .

This **WHITE** finger says : To have a new, clean life, you need to receive **JESUS CHRIST** as your **SAVIOR**.

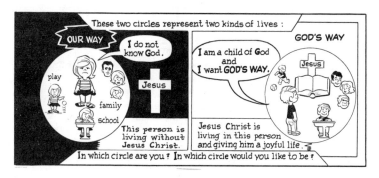

These two circles represent two kinds of lives :

OUR WAY

I do not know God .

play
family
school
Jesus

This person is living without Jesus Christ.

GOD'S WAY

I am a child of God and I want **GOD'S WAY**.

Jesus

Jesus Christ is living in this person and giving him a joyful life.

In which circle are you ? In which circle would you like to be ?

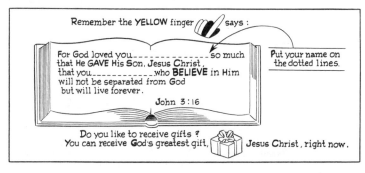

Remember the **YELLOW** finger says :

For God loved you _ _ _ _ _ _ _ _ _ _ _ _ so much that He **GAVE** His Son, Jesus Christ, that you _ _ _ _ _ _ _ _ _ _ who **BELIEVE** in Him will not be separated from God but will live forever.

John 3:16

Put your name on the dotted lines.

Do you like to receive gifts ?
You can receive God's greatest gift, Jesus Christ, right now.

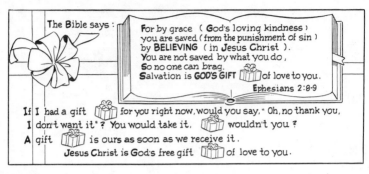

The Bible says:

> For by grace (God's loving kindness)
> you are saved (from the punishment of sin)
> by **BELIEVING** (in Jesus Christ).
> You are not saved by what you do,
> So no one can brag.
> Salvation is **GOD'S GIFT** of love to you.
>
> Ephesians 2:8-9

If I had a gift for you right now, would you say, " Oh, no thank you,
I don't want it"? You would take it, wouldn't you?
A gift is ours as soon as we receive it.
Jesus Christ is God's free gift of love to you.

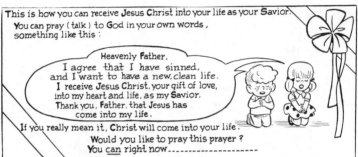

This is how you can receive Jesus Christ into your life as your Savior.
You can pray (talk) to God in your own words,
something like this:

> Heavenly Father,
> I agree that I have sinned,
> and I want to have a new, clean life.
> I receive Jesus Christ, your gift of love,
> into my heart and life, as my Savior.
> Thank you, Father, that Jesus has
> come into my life.

If you really mean it, Christ will come into your life.
Would you like to pray this prayer?
You can right now..........................

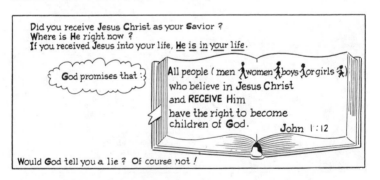

Did you receive Jesus Christ as your Savior?
Where is He right now?
If you received Jesus into your life, **He is in your life.**

God promises that:

> All people (men women boys or girls)
> who believe in Jesus Christ
> and **RECEIVE** Him
> have the right to become
> children of God.
>
> John 1:12

Would God tell you a lie? Of course not!

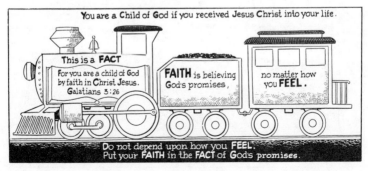

You are a Child of God if you received Jesus Christ into your life.

This is a **FACT**
For you are a child of God
by faith in Christ Jesus.
Galatians 3:26

FAITH is believing
God's promises,

no matter how
you **FEEL.**

Do not depend upon how you **FEEL.**
Put your **FAITH** in the **FACT** of God's promises.

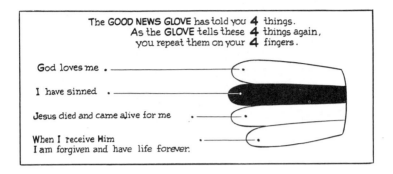

In sharing Christ with a child, a number of principles apply. First, choose a good time to talk with your child, preferably when he is rested and relaxed. Second, it is important that God has prepared the child's heart to hear the gospel. Prayer for the child's understanding is vital. Third, emphasize the death and resurrection of Christ, presenting it clearly and as an act of highest love. Fourth, have the child pray aloud with you to receive Christ. Then review with the child what he has just done.

After Vonette had invited Jesus Christ into her life, she had another important lesson to learn, one that was essential for being a good mother. "For years I strove to be a good Christian. I tried to live the Christian life in my own strength. I tried to do the right thing. In fact I almost made myself ill trying to live the life Christ had called me to."

And then one day Vonette realized that the Christian life was more than difficult, It was impossible! "God didn't want me to live the Christian life in my own strength. He wanted to live his life for me, in me, and through me. He would do it all. It was my responsibility to trust and obey him."

This was new realization for Vonette. It took time to put this new truth into application in her life. She learned that either she herself would be in control of her life—or she could by an act of her will, give her life into the control of Christ. "To take one step," she now explains, "is the single most important thing for a Christian mother to do. For a mother in her own strength can do no more than the natural. But if a mother lets God rule her life, she can use his strength, his wisdom, his authority and power to have a supernatural effect in her home. This is what every mother needs!"

In the Bright home on occasion they have what they call a "throne check." "Are you in control of your life? Or is Christ on the throne of your life?" "And at very inappropriate times," Vonette states, "my sons have a way of asking that question of *me!* I am sorry to say that there have been times when I have to confess to them, 'No, son, Christ is not on the throne of my life. Will you pray with me once again that I will give him control?' "

The "Good News Comic Book" offers a cartoon feature to explain to a young child how to keep Christ in control of his life.

"If Christ is on the throne of each person's life at our house, things work in harmony. For Christ never wars against himself. But if he is in control of my sons' lives, but I am in control of my life—there is discord. If we all are in control of our own lives, there is civil war in our home!

"We have learned to have this 'throne check' because it has helped us all to keep our perspective." One evening when the Brights were saying their prayers together, Dr. Bright asked his then eight-year-old son, Zac, "Who is on the throne of your life?" He said, "Jesus." He asked his then five-year-old son, Brad, who was on the throne of his life. He too answered, "Jesus."

The next morning, their mother had prepared for breakfast a special dish called "egg in a bonnet." It was a delicious thick piece of French toast with a hole in the middle and in that hole was a poached egg. As he was enjoying it, Dr. Bright looked over at Brad. He was not eating the egg nor the toast.

Dr. Bright said, "Brad, eat your breakfast."

"I don't want it," he answered.

"Of course you do. You'll enjoy it. Look at me. I'm enjoying mine," returned Bill.

"Well," he said, "I don't like it and I'm not going to eat it." And being a bit dramatic he began to release a few tears.

Dr. Bright had to make up his mind what he was going to do. He finally decided that he could either say, "Now, young man, you eat that breakfast or I'll spank you," or "Forget it, I'll eat it myself."

Dr. Bright, however, thought of a better idea. "Brad, who is on the throne of your life this morning?" At that, the tears really began to pour. The boy understood the point that his father was trying to make. He had been taught the concept that Christ must be on the throne; but Christ was not on the throne of his life at that moment. When Brad regained his composure, he replied, "The devil and me."

Dr. Bright asked, "Whom do you want on the throne?"

"Jesus," he answered.

So, Dr. Bright suggested that they pray together. Brad prayed, "Dear Jesus, forgive me for being disobedient and help me to like this egg." God heard that prayer; and Brad enjoyed his breakfast.

That evening as the Brights were saying their prayers, Dr. Bright asked Brad who had been on the throne of his life that day, and he said, "Jesus." "Oh," he added, "except at breakfast this morning."

This illustration shows that a very young child can learn a personal and consistent walk with the Lord. In fact, to obey Jesus as King is the next lesson after salvation and assurance of salvation that should be taught to a child.

One reason that Brad Bright was receptive to his father's authority may be Bill Bright's open heart policy. Dr. Bright travels a great deal, which means he is away from home almost three-fourths of the year. So when he is away he calls often and shares his love with his family. But when he is at home, it is well known around Campus Crusade for Christ headquarters that two boys, Zachary and Brad Bright, are free to interrupt the president of Campus Crusade at any time. Whether Bill is in a board meeting, a conversation, or any situation, the boys know that their problems, needs, and desire to talk with their dad always comes first. What a living illustration to these boys of a loving heavenly Father who always makes himself accessible to our every situation.

Another lesson Vonette had to learn is called "Availability." "Most mothers have a sense of inadequacy. 'What can the world do with the likes of me,' they ask, 'when I can't even settle my own problems?'" Vonette points out that the great men and women of the Bible were inadequate persons: Joseph a slave, Moses a wanderer, David a shepherd, Peter a fisherman, Ruth a Moabite widow, Deborah a housewife and prophetess, and Paul, who confessed to being the worst of sinners.

"Mothers are standing in a good tradition, for God chooses the weak things of the world to illustrate his power. To be available to God releases him to control our circumstances and finances, to give us wisdom, strength, and creative ideas." According to Mrs. Bright the Lord doesn't ask for great women, just women who are willing to follow him. "All I need is *you*," says the Lord.

Availability means to Vonette that she is willing to wash diapers with a good attitude if that is what the Lord asks of her. "I'm available to do the laundry when I would rather be going out speaking or doing some activity which the world terms success. I'm available to have my husband gone for long periods of time. I'm available to meet the needs of my teen-age sons. And most of all, I'm available for interruptions. "Lord, you just show me how to handle them.' "

To Vonette's amazement she has watched how God has taken her availability to him and made the things she didn't want to do become something that produced great joy. She has been available to see resentment turn to praise, self-pity turn to a healthy attitude toward herself and others. She has seen giving replace selfishness, and love replace indifference.

Vonette remembers a time early in her marriage, when Christians came to their home for a meeting. The young people were learning how to share their faith, and Vonette longed to be out participating with them. Instead she was finishing up the dishes in the kitchen and endeavoring to get two active boys to bed.

"How I resented being trapped in the kitchen," she said. "I had to fight the bitterness in my heart." But after years of this kind of struggle Vonette finally learned that resistance to the will of God was not the road to peace.

"I found that if I prayed, 'Lord, change my attitude and give me a heart for scraping fried chicken out of the bottom of the frying pan'; 'Please help me accept the task of removing the ring from the bathtub'; 'Help me to enjoy my time with curious, questioning little boys'; these are the kinds of prayers that God loves to answer.

"And after many years I have decided that if I can serve Christ more and honor him more in my life by doing the prosaic tasks and chores of a home—cleaning a toilet bowl, dusting the furniture, unstopping the garbage disposal for the eighth time—than I can by doing the glamorous things, then I will choose Christ. Because," she concludes, "great blessing and inner joy are the results of serving him."

Learning to call on God for wisdom is another lesson that Vonette has welcomed. James 1:5 (TLB) states, "If you want to know what God wants you to do, ask him, and he will gladly tell you, for he is always ready to give a bountiful supply of wisdom to all who ask him; he will not resent it." Vonette believes that drawing on God's wisdom is the key to communication with young people. "We need to let God show us exactly what to do."

One afternoon when Mrs. Bright had come home from several days in Miami, Zachary, by then in high school, had decided that his teacher had given him an unreasonable assignment. Rather than doing it he determined that he would take the class over again. Vonette explained that if he took the class again it meant she would have to pick him up at three o'clock every afternoon for the next six weeks. This was difficult for her to schedule and she asked Zac to reconsider it. To this he replied, "I'll ride my bike. I don't mind."

As mother and son talked, Vonette inevitably sought the Lord's wisdom. It came to her mind that Zachary needed to learn obedience in a difficult situation. He needed to learn to trust God under tough authority. That evening at family devotions Vonette explained to Zachary, "As I prayed today, I decided that God wants you to finish that class. I've talked with your teacher and you can still turn the assignment in on Monday."

"Mother," said Zac, "if I worked around the clock I couldn't finish that assignment by Monday."

"Well, let's pray about it."

"It doesn't matter how much you pray about it," replied Zac. "The assignment is just too hard and I can't do it."

Vonette noted that it wasn't the most intimate prayer they ever had, but she was sure that it was God's direction to see that Zachary finished his assignment. She added to Zachary, "You can stay home from work tomorrow and get the assignment done." But as she left the room the Lord reminded her that Zac wouldn't be learning responsibility and obedience if he neglected one job for another. So she turned back and explained to Zac that she had spoken too quickly. "You will have to go to work tomorrow. But I expect you to get the assignment done."

That night as she went to bed, she asked God to intervene and help convince her son of the rightness of her decision. And in the morning Zachary apologized. "I'm sorry about my attitude, Mom," he told her. "I believe God does want me to finish this assignment. So after I come home from work today I'll work around the clock and try to get it done."

That evening when Zac came home, Vonette sat him down at his desk and made sure he had plenty of hot chocolate and cookies. She was careful to check on him from time to time with encouraging words. By Monday morning the assignment was complete and at the end of the day Zachary walked in the front door grinning from ear to ear. "I made the highest grade in the class."

"Zac learned a lesson from this," replied Vonette. "But I learned an even greater lesson in terms of letting God show me exactly what to do." As a mother, Vonette is grateful for God's promise that "if you want to know what God wants you to do, simply ask!"

One thought that Vonette Bright would like to pass on to mothers more than anything else is this: "What this world needs are godly mothers who will get on their knees for the cause of Jesus Christ." With all the duties of a housewife it may seem that she doesn't play an important role in the world. But Vonette believes that the woman at home with children can be quietly changing the world through godly intercession.

"Pray over the kitchen sink, pray while gardening, pray as you sew. A mother's prayers as she does her daily chores can change legislation, cause a business deal to go through for her husband, stimulate the PTA to make a pertinent decision, send the gospel to foreign lands, bring the right people into her children's life, carry encouragement and hope to many, and on and on. Never, never, underestimate the world-changing effects brought about by prayer."

Along with prayer, Vonette sees other important tasks for women. First, she encourages women to share their faith in Jesus Christ. Many courses in how to witness are available; a woman who seeks to make her life count fully for Christ will avail herself of them. At the laundromat, the supermarket, the beauty parlor, the cleaners, in a department store or at numerous meetings or activities, she can inoffensively pass on the most important truth in the world: that God loves people and has a marvelous plan for their individual lives, made possible by Jesus Christ.

As the children nap she can have a friend in for coffee and tell her the good news of salvation. Or she can have a weekly or biweekly Bible study. Her Christian neighbor can take care of the mothers' children, and she herself can present a simple study on a book from the Bible on some Christian subject, and influence many needy women.

A woman can pray for wisdom to counsel a friend. She can speak words of encouragement to troubled lives over the telephone. A Sunday school class may appeal to some. Giving or helping others may be an outlet for her Christian faith. In regard to public issues, a woman can write letters to TV stations, newspapers, magazines, legislators, expressing praise or disgust for specific ideas presented. She can write to the board of education, or take a PTA office.

Vonette does caution that a woman should carefully pray about which activities outside of the home the Lord would have her be involved in. It does little good to help the world and lose your own children. "I used to spend more time away from home speaking and leading groups. But since my children have been teen-agers I realize they need me now more than ever. I've had to limit my time away from home."

But while Vonette is at home, she seeks to utilize fully the opportunities God gives her. In fact she is able to look at mundane chores with a bit of optimism and humor. Over her kitchen sink, a sign one foot high and six feet wide reads:

LET MY CELESTIAL KNOWLEDGE AFFECT MY
DOMESTIC DUTIES!

Seven
Marianne Staubach

Before Marianne married Roger Staubach, the Dallas Cowboys football star, she had a number of ideas on rearing children. Watching other boys and girls carry on in a grocery store she thought to herself, "My children will never do that!"

Her idea of a well-behaved child was one who stood close by his mother's side, robot style, smiling sweetly. "But," she says, "I've learned that children aren't like that!" They have a lot of rambunctiousness and natural childish curiosity. Now, with her three young girls in a grocery store, her only rule is "Look, but do not touch." "Actually I almost have nightmares of an entire rack coming crashing down into the aisles. So I feel if I succeed in just this one rule, I'm doing a fairly good job."

The Staubach children are delightful little girls of six, four, and three, and their mother has many thoughts to share with new mothers. The Staubachs are trying to teach their children several things while they are young. One is confidence. When Jennifer first started school she was hesitant, shy, and fearful (much like Mrs. Staubach as a child). To help compensate for this, her parents tried to point out all the exciting things that could happen to her in school, all the good times

Marianne Staubach is wife of pro athlete Roger Staubach, quarterback for the Dallas Cowboys. The Staubachs have three daughters and live in Dallas, Texas.

that were ahead. At the same time they let her know that some of the other children were just as afraid as she was. Mrs. Staubach also made a practice of walking Jennifer to school for a while, until they found a friend who could accompany her and likewise give her assurance.

Another thing the Staubachs are teaching their children is to share. They encourage the child to look beyond herself and see the needs of others. Children are born self-centered. Their only orientation is to themselves. When they cry, for example, they have no sense of their mother's tiredness or hectic schedule.

Mrs. Staubach recalls her own mother, who reared five children. She showed her unselfishness by putting her own needs after those of her children. "Not that she catered to us, but she did take time to do things that would teach us. And I learned in that large family that a child must give as well as take. I found this to be good training in later life, when I could more easily accept defeat than some children who had no brothers or sisters. And I can see this now with my own girls. Having sisters will work to their advantage. They have to learn they don't always get their own way. For example, when Jennifer comes in and wants to tell me something, she has to learn to wait until I'm finished talking to Michelle. This is all part of learning sharing and unselfishness."

Jennifer at age six is more apt to get her feelings hurt than Stephanie, who is three. This is because Jennifer is gaining awareness of the outside world. People have become more important to her and thus she senses their approval and disapproval. Because a child's needs for parental approval are so great, parental displeasure may be the surest source of motivation toward unselfishness.

Once a child begins to see the need to think of others and share with them, the source of giving will be found in Christ. A parent should encourage the child to ask God for extra love for the moody friend down the street; for the generosity to share a toy; or for the helpful attitude to pray for and say nice things to needy schoolmates. "I feel you can't teach a child too early to think about others."

In these early years the Staubachs are also trying to teach responsibility. Making beds is one of the daily chores in their home, and getting the sheets and covers to go just right can sometimes be frustrating to a five- or six-year-old. They tend to leave wrinkles in the covers. "I find that the best thing here," says Mrs. Staubach, "is to praise their *efforts* whether the *job* is done perfectly or not. Sometimes I say, 'Boy, you sure do a fine job on your bed. I bet if we just pull this one corner here it will be perfect.' Our object is to be sure that we leave a good feeling with the child about her accomplishments so that she'll be encouraged to take more responsibility. We feel you just can't praise a child's efforts enough."

A goal of the Staubach home is to give love and acceptance to their young girls. "Each one of our children is unique," says Marianne. "Jennifer is medium as far as being quiet or outgoing. She is middle of the road when it comes to meeting people—shy at first, but she does come out and speak to people. Michelle, the second child, is very quiet and introverted. The first three weeks of school she would hardly talk with the nursery school teacher. Although she isn't verbal, she is quite aware of what's going on. And Stephanie, the youngest girl, is really relaxed. She's a chatterbox. In the nursery school she's the first to volunteer for anything.

"With all of our children, Roger and I want to be able to communicate that we love each child for what she is herself. This doesn't mean that we treat our children all alike, because their needs are different. But we do try to take each child as she is and give her plenty of acceptance. We hope to teach by this that certain personalities or temperaments have no special status with God. It makes no difference to him whether we're outspoken or retiring. What is important is our love, faith, and obedience to Christ.

"In these early years of rearing children I am finding that my three girls mimic me. They all carry purses, because I carry a purse. If I put makeup on, they want to wear makeup. And my shoes, though they are many sizes bigger than their feet, are constantly being used by them. No doubt the mimicking shows up in attitudes as well as behavior. If they're prone to imitate mother's bad habits, hopefully they're going to imitate my desire to please God and live for him as well.

"In this area of imitation we have tried to set examples for the children along certain lines. One goal is to project a happy attitude. I've noticed that if I come into a room with a bad attitude, within ten minutes the children are cross and irritable with each other. But if I come into a room with a cheerful and positive countenance, peace and tranquility seem to reign in our home. It's just evidence to me that good moods or bad moods are picked up by children. It makes me so conscious of keeping my thought-life pleasing to God.

"Children also imitate the way their parents treat other people. I've learned, through reading a noted psychologist, that children will be to each other as the parents are to the child." The statement of the psychologist was that many times a stranger or friend will come into the home and the parent will tell the child to go away because he or she is busy talking to the outsider. This makes it obvious to the child that when others are around, she takes an inferior position. She is not *special*, even though she is in her *own* home. "If you give respect to outsiders in the home," says the psychologist, "how much more essential it is to give respect to your children's needs in the home." And so, even if you are with a neighbor, or if you are very busy, and your child comes up and asks for attention or assurance of your love, or wants to share something with you, excuse yourself from your friend or your task for just a minute and meet the needs of that child.

"I have found that when I am busy in the kitchen, and really can't talk to the children because I'm taking a hot pan out of the oven or I'm right in the middle of something, I can say to that child, 'Mommy's busy, but I do want very much to talk with you. If you'll just wait until Mommy gets dinner on the table, then I can sit down with you to hear what you have to say.' The point that I have learned from this is the imitation factor. If the children see that I respect them, they in turn tend to respect other people's rights as well."

Recently the girls have begun to need more than just cuddling and assurances of love. Now their emotions and personality problems need to be dealt with. "One thing that has helped me with this," says Mrs. Staubach, "is getting as much preparation as possible by reading books or by talking to other mothers about the stages a child will go through. This helps me not to feel guilty when problems come and not to worry excessively about them."

When one of the girls was two, she had a problem of picking her nose. Mrs. Staubach felt this might be a steady habit in her life, but she grew out of it. When Jennifer was six she took on a very stubborn spirit as she left home for grammar school. "It helps me to know that these things will pass, and to realize that God will help me deal with whatever problem comes up."

It is important for a mother to use her mind as well as her prayers in figuring out what the child is trying to tell her. "When Jennifer is crabby I sometimes wonder if school isn't going well for her or if she has a deeper need that's not being met. I try to ask reasonable questions to bring out what might be bothering her so that the problem won't persist. But this takes a lot of time with her to get to know her personality well. Studying a child is something like studying a textbook."

Marianne also believes it is just as important for her to understand her own emotions as those of her children. "When my fourth child was due, Stephanie was only one-and-a-half years old. And so several months before the birth I tried to prepare Stephanie for her independence. I took her pacifier away from her. I taught her to drink from a cup instead of a bottle. And I encouraged her to do many of the things that I had been doing for her."

The delivery of the baby was traumatic. She was stillborn. Mrs. Staubach was left with natural cravings to cuddle a child and to baby someone. "Subconsciously I was looking for a replacement for the baby I lost. I caught myself rocking and carrying Stephanie more. I began doing things for her that she had learned to do for herself. But I soon realized that this wasn't really helping either Stephanie or me. I know that God was giving me an understanding of my own reactions so that I didn't carry it too far—to the point that it hurt Stephanie or myself."

Good and positive feelings about God should be implanted during a child's early years. "We try to make our children aware of God by talking about him. We bring up such ideas as, 'God loves you very much,' or 'God made you, and he cares about you.' To help orient them to pleasing God we make statements like, 'When we do this it makes God happy,' or 'When we do this it makes God unhappy.' In fact, we've often used this idea when the children are arguing. Even though they had heard many times that God isn't pleased when they fight with each other, the lesson was like water off a duck's back. Then one afternoon in the midst of an argument we heard Jennifer reprimand the other children. 'You're not making God happy,' she said." Teaching children that they should please God will inevitably show them that they fail at this. And this may be the parents' opening to share that Christ died on the cross to forgive their personal sins.

"We encourage our little girls with the truth that God is everywhere. The child then understands that God is always available to help us. His love and protection are all around us. This can be tremendously reassuring to a child. We explain to the children that even though they can't see God, they can see the things he does. This gives them assurance that he is there. Just like the wind. We can't see the wind, but we can see the effect of the wind on the trees and how it helps the birds in flight."

Nowhere is God's presence more real to the Staubach children than in their prayer time. The parents teach the girls that God hears every word no matter how softly spoken. And he knows and understands the thoughts inside them even if they are not spoken. "We have a Catholic background," says Marianne. "In our home we use a mixture of memorized prayer and what we call free-form prayer. Roger and I encourage the children just to talk to God—to thank him and ask him for their needs. In this way we share a loving God nightly and individually with each of our children.

"Of course, since our children are all under seven, we need to keep concepts of God very simple. They take childish needs to God, as when at Halloween Stephanie prayed, 'God, I'm sick. Help me to get well so I can go trick-or-treating.'

"And we encourage the children to remember things during the day to ask God about or to thank him for." A typical prayer time included, "Thank you for the day and for letting me go to my friend's house. Help me to share my toys. Thank you for my new dress."

"It can go on and on," says Marianne. "In fact, one of our girls goes through such a detailed and lengthy list, I often wonder if she is just trying to delay bedtime."

Along with a prayer time that is as natural and commonplace as if they were talking to one another, in the rest of their Christian faith, the Staubachs stress relationship to God, not ritual. They enjoy praising God as a family in church on Sundays as an expression of their faith.

When it comes to teaching small children spiritual principles, here are some helps that may be beneficial for young mothers. First, proceed from the known to the unknown. This means to use an example of something a child is familiar with and relate it to a spiritual truth. When talking to a child about sin and his need for salvation in Christ, a mother could point out that sin is like a stain on a piece of cloth. The cloth may be good but the stain has soiled it. Stain remover is like the blood of Christ that cleanses us from sin. As a mother says this she can have the cloth and stain remover with her, demonstrating it to the child. In this way a child has a vivid picture to help her understand and retain a spiritual truth.

Second, don't assume that a child has really understood what you're talking about. It's helpful to ask a child to repeat the story back to you. A mother could say, "Now you tell me the story. I bet you can tell it just as well as I can." This will help the mother to note what the child has missed or misinterpreted.

Third, ask stimulating questions. In telling the story of David and Goliath, a mother could say, "Now what do you like about this story? Why do you think God used David?"

The point is to get them to think the story through for themselves.

Fourth, use repetition. The more times a child hears a truth the more apt she is to get it into her understanding. If it is cemented well enough into her mind at an early age, it will serve her throughout her life.

Fifth, take the child's questions, statements, and ideas seriously. It is important to praise her for any good thinking that she is doing. Be careful in handling wrong conclusions by saying, "You're almost right." Or, "Well, I guess that could be possible, but let's find out some more about it." Don't offend the child when correcting her. This will encourage her to talk and be involved. It will keep the door open for more teaching.

Sixth, use your imagination. Help the child to visualize or feel what she is learning. A child will quickly lose interest unless exciting words, vivid pictures, or elements of adventure and humor are used.

A child learns more quickly if she herself is involved in the story. Children may act out roles, such as in the story of Daniel in the lions' den. One child may be the king who sentences Daniel, one child may be Daniel, and another child may play a lion. Some of the parts may be imagined. But this entails little more than reading through the Bible portions and instructing the child to recite lines or perform actions as the story goes along. Costumes or props may be added.

Another way to get a child involved is to use clay, crayons, or water colors to create the story herself as you tell it. Flannelgraphs or chalk drawings are also helpful aids.

Seventh, don't overeducate a child. It's better to give her small doses at a time. Answer only the questions she asks. Don't bore the child. When she begins to get restless, you should change the subject, insert a new idea, or suggest that you take a break for cookies and milk.

Last, be willing to learn from your children. It gives a child a wonderful feeling if she can provide a thought that is beneficial to you. Parents should let their child know that she has helped them with a good thought or a spiritual insight.

The Staubachs work hard to communicate with their girls. One situation came up when the stillbirth of their fourth child needed to be explained to the children. As far as Mrs. Staubach knew, her pregnancy for the whole nine months had been in order. There were no complications until labor began. She was in the hospital an hour and a half before delivery took place. During this time the doctor found the amniotic fluid to be discolored. There was no heartbeat from the baby. The physician told them there was little possibility that the baby was alive.

"I felt that this was the goodness of God in giving me a little time to prepare myself—but not a lot of time to dwell on the fact," Marianne said.

Marianne was not allowed to see the baby. She couldn't even imagine what the child might have looked like because her three girls don't resemble each other. "This," she said, "was again the grace of God to spare me a vivid memory of a dead little girl."

Roger was waiting for her after the delivery. Their first words to each other were, "It's God's will." "We were both crying and upset, but we were able to accept the fact that it was up to God, not us. God had good reason for this to happen. Our great consolation was in our Christian faith. We knew our baby girl was in heaven. We would see her again. And it was this fact that Roger, alone, had to communicate to our three girls."

Roger came home and took the girls into the bedroom. With tears in his eyes he explained that God had chosen to take their new little sister to be in heaven with him. This was a great honor, he told them. The baby would never suffer. And someday they could all be together.

"We weren't sure at the time if our children understood this," says Mrs. Staubach. "We did know that it was important for them to see that God is a loving God—that he had taken the child because he wanted her, not because he wanted to hurt us."

A year or so later one of the girls who was only three at the time the baby died asked, "Do old people die?"

"Yes, they do."

"Our baby must have been awfully old," suggested Michelle. Mrs. Staubach explained that people died when God knew they were ready to be taken. Young or old, this was the best time to die.

"I know," Marianne recalled, "an experience like this isn't something that's soon forgotten. All I could do during the time was pray that God would help me get through just one more day. I continued to reassure myself in the goodness of God who knows best. He knew better than I. And it's true that time does heal a broken heart.

"The hardest experience was to stay in the hospital the following day. The baby had to be taken in a small casket by Roger and our parish priest to the cemetery. This was so difficult for my husband. But again Christ gave real sustenance to triumph over the problems that everyone will experience.

"I know that in the future I will wonder at different times what this little girl may have been like or how things would have been if she had lived. On what would have been her birthday, I became very sentimental. One of the girls brought up the subject and it made it a very difficult day. However, faith carries us through.

"One great help in rearing our children is the closeness that Roger and I have together. We try to discuss each thing, to figure out a plan of attack or course of action for the children. When Michelle was transferred to a larger bed she refused to stay there. We would often find her sleeping on the floor by the door of the den. Roger and I talked it over. We decided that discipline with love was the right way to handle the problem. Between the two of us we concluded that Michelle would be spanked every time she got out of bed. Once we had settled the question, it was less difficult to follow through. We then didn't have to discuss the problem each time it came up."

So for the next two weeks when Michelle got out of bed, she got a spanking. She averaged six spankings a night, but that settled it. To this day Michelle has never gotten out of her bed without calling Mom or Dad first.

"In working as a team, Roger and I try to discuss a problem together. Then we decide how both of us should handle the situation. We have tried to ward off problems before they arise by explaining to the child what Mommy and Daddy expect of them. This is important for a child's security.

"Our motivation for working well as a team is our love for one another, and our love for God. The greatest gift we can give our children is a heritage of Christian love."

Eight
Anita Bryant

For a girl who came from a broken home and lived with various relatives much of her life, Anita Bryant, otherwise known as Mrs. Bob Green, is doing a fine job rearing her four children. It just goes to prove that one home needn't repeat another home's mistakes.

Anita and Bob give Christ all the credit for their happy family. "It was when I was eight years old," says Anita, "during the time when my parents were happy and their faith rested on Christ, that both my sister and I made the decision of inviting Jesus Christ to come into our lives. I've often thought that, if my parents had continued to put the Lord first, their breakup and ultimate divorce would have been prevented. And I also wonder how much stronger I could have been in the Lord, and how many mistakes could have been prevented in my young life, had my parents persevered in the direction of living Christ-centered lives."

Most people have seen Anita Bryant's family in the Florida Citrus Orange Juice presentation on television. And so it

---

Anita Bryant (Mrs. Robert Green) does more than make orange juice commercials. She is the mother of four, is a professional singing and recording star, and has written several books, including Amazing Grace, Bless This House, Light My Candle, *and* Mine Eyes Have Seen the Glory. *Her husband is also her business manager.*

could be said that the entire family is in show business. Yet here as well as in the church they maintain a vibrant Christian testimony.

Some people have suggested to Anita that her faith in Christ is a crutch. "It's not a crutch. It's a platform—something out of rock that I can stand on, that holds me up."

As the Greens rub shoulders with movie stars and TV personalities, they observe the lack of peace and substance in many of their lives. They see the struggle of children from unhappy marriages and the superficial atmosphere within the homes. Anita attributes the superficial quality to either ignorance or indifference to spiritual things. "Christ is the solid rock that I stand on. He alone gives peace and stability and motivation, which I need day by day."

One question the Greens ask many people they meet is, "Are you satisfied? Have you found the inner something that you have been searching for all your life?"

"I know that I have!" Anita affirms. "When you find Christ you know that you've found what you have always been looking for. And nothing can take him away. Even if you are weak, your platform is strong. Christ can hold you up."

Marriage to Bob brought a new dimension to Anita's relationship with God. Before she married she knew how crucial it was that Bob know Christ as his Savior. "I've watched it over and over again. It takes two, not just one committed Christian parent, to have an abundant home life." It was only moments before their marriage that Bob did commit his full life to Christ and they covenanted together to have a Christian home.

Perhaps the greatest test of her Christian faith came when Anita became pregnant with her third child. When labor began about two and a half months before the due date, it was discovered that she was expecting twins. Anita knew that the twins were in great danger and that her life was on the line as well. Many transfusions were needed to keep her alive.

After the twins' birth it was thought that they might not live. Or if they did live, there might be considerable brain damage. During this time, friends and admirers wrote of their support and prayers. Mr. and Mrs. Green now call them their "miracle babies." The twins not only lived, but their bodies and minds are normal. At this point the Greens realized again that their lives and the lives of their children were totally dependent on God's grace.

"I didn't start out in life as a strong Christian," says Anita. "In fact, I'm painfully aware of my own inadequacies, my temper, my shortcomings, my inconsistencies. But again I've learned that 'even if I am weak, Christ can be my strength.' " That verse, Philippians 4:13, is her favorite Scripture.

Anita looks at the Christian life as a plant. When you first invite Jesus Christ into your heart to be your Savior, the seed is planted. Then the seed is watered by three things: reading the Bible, prayer, and Christian fellowship (in a local Bible-teaching church). The little plant begins to grow and God begins to remove the weeds about the plant. "There are plenty of areas in a Christian's life that need weeding. As I confess my sins to God, he helps me to overcome these problem areas.

"I have found all my answers as a wife and as a mother in the Word of God. For the person who doesn't know Christ, the Bible spells out the gospel. They need to understand that Christ came into the world to take on himself their sins—past, present, and future. Through the pages of his historic and supernatural book, God's Holy Word, they can read Christ's invitations to them of eternal relationship with himself. This is what I did at age eight: I heeded his voice and received him into my heart (see John 1:12).

"For those of us who have received Christ, it's important to take the next step. Eternal life is guaranteed for all who come to Christ. But abundant life is left to those who fully commit their lives to Christ, who decide that Christ will have final say in every decision of their life."

One of Anita's greatest problems is selfishness. She's a woman with a great deal of drive, stemming from her part-Cherokee, part-Irish, and part-Scottish background. She has had a hard time realizing that Christ needs to make her every decision. At the same time she has had difficulty seeing that her husband is the leader of their home. In both areas she has had to submit her own will to a greater authority.

"Women's true liberation," says Anita, "is being liberated from ourselves. I have found complete liberation in Christ." Unfortunately Anita didn't learn in her young years the fact that she had everything she needed in Christ. She had to learn many lessons the hard way, and some not so long ago.

"As a mother," she says, "I want my children to have what I missed as a child. Already my children are ahead of where I was at their age. The greatest thrill in the world is to watch our children mature in Christ."

One thing that has greatly benefited the Green home is a prayer altar. They got the idea from Senator Mark Hatfield and his wife, who use an altar as the center of their family. One day Bob surprised Anita by finding a similar altar and bringing it home. The antique prayer altar sits in the center of Mom and Dad's master bedroom-sittingroom providing a quiet and out-of-the-way place where the family can come together or individuals can seek and find the Lord. "Any family can make an altar. It doesn't matter what size it is or the materials it's made from or it can be a place set aside like your living room sofa. But what is important is that it is designed for the purpose of worshiping and talking to God.

"You can learn many things about your children when you pray with them. Things that they don't often confide because of lack of time or just because it's so personal will be revealed when they talk to their heavenly Father."

At the end of each day when the children and the parents gather at the prayer altar Anita asks for forgiveness for the times she has yelled at the children or failed to do things as she should, or done other things that she shouldn't have. When the children hear their parents honestly bare their sins to the Lord, it not only makes the child more accepting of the parents' weaknesses, but it also encourages the children to be honest with the Lord about their own shortcomings.

Sometimes at the prayer altar when spankings haven't been administered in the right spirit the Greens hear prayers such as "Forgive me for my sins. And forgive Mommy and Daddy for being so cranky." One time Anita got very angry with Gloria about something; she lost her temper and gave Gloria a hard spanking. The little girl cried as Mommy stalked off and then later came to Anita saying, "Mommy, I forgive you."

"We try to make a point of telling our children that we aren't perfect. At times we may punish them for things they didn't do or get angry with them when it really isn't their fault." "It's because we are human," she says to them, "and far from being flawless." Again, sometimes after the kids have been disciplined for a small thing they didn't do, or for something unimportant, Bobby looks at Mom and says, "Well, nobody's perfect." "And," says Anita, "you have to agree with that!

"The children really don't think less of us for acknowledging our sins to God. They actually seem to love us more. It creates a stronger bond between us by showing that we are all in the same boat—sinners in need of God's grace.

"My greatest prayer is for consistency. My nature is basically inconsistent. I change from sweet to hot-tempered in seconds. And I can see the confusion and frustration this creates for my husband and my children.

"And I'm often so exacting with my family. Everything has to run just like I've got it planned. I don't naturally leave much room for flexing and considering the moods and needs of my home. On church mornings I used to become a tyrant. I would start early. The children had to be dressed for Sunday school. Everything had to move on schedule and most everything was left up to me. The very day that I should have had extra love and understanding for my family, I was yelling more than ever at the kids and hardly speaking to Bob. For a while I really felt it was Bob and the children's fault. I mean, I really did! It seems that nobody would be getting ready for church. And so I would rush the children so much that by the time everybody was in the car we were all in a foul mood." Even on the drive to church, Anita fussed at Bob while she put on her earrings and lipstick and brushed her eyebrows. The babies would be crying in the back seat. Bobby and Billy would be fighting.

As her husband observed this, his reaction was: "As soon as we get to church you turn into a goody-goody. You want to hold my hand and act lovey-dovey. But what about on the way to church? Why can't you be nice? And when we get up in the morning, why can't you be nice then?"

This thought kept bugging Anita because she knew there was truth in it. Finally the Lord got through to her. The trouble on Sundays was her own fault, not that of her husband and children. God showed her that she had to stop blaming the family. She needed to get her own life in order in terms of calmness and patience.

And so, after Christ helped Anita to see her need, she began rushing out of bed each Sunday morning. But this time it was with the purpose of praying for the right attitude. "In fact," she said, "I have gotten so I start Sundays the Saturday night before." Saturday night at the prayer altar she brought her petitions of need to the Lord. As one psychiatrist observes, "It's not the problems of others that bother people so much, but their refusal to face up to their sins." And so with Anita's open confession before the family, the children were able to understand their mom's problem better and were more willing to cooperate with her.

"Change wasn't easy. Many of the changes in my life have been difficult and time-consuming. But several weeks after I began praying specifically about Sunday mornings, Bob commented that he had really noticed a difference."

In thinking further of her inconsistency, Anita thinks that her second biggest problem is intolerance. "I know how to stick a knife in where it really hurts. And often, because of my busy schedule I say things without thinking. The results are hurt feelings. For a long time I tried to deal with this problem by controlling my tongue. Then, growing as a Christian, I realized that my wagging tongue was a result of my undisciplined mind. It wasn't my tongue I needed to control. It was my thinking pattern." She began to perceive that her mind needed to be renewed daily with the Word of God, and she needed the self-control of the Holy Spirit to give her a sound mentality that wouldn't result in alarming words.

"It takes time to retrain your thoughts. And it takes careful guarding of them. But part of the mental gymnastics of reorienting our thought-life is in understanding our enemy.

"Of course, the Bible says that every person who knows Christ as Savior has three enemies—the world, the flesh, and the devil. And I'm not blaming everything on the devil. What I am saying is that he uses the world and my own flesh to accomplish his goals in defeating the work of God. And I know that Satan works overtime on *mothers.* Because if he can destroy the home, he's pretty well destroyed the church and the ministry of the church. Satan would like nothing better than to see me get into despair about my life and my home. And I believe with all my heart that understanding the subtleties of Satan in our home and world is paramount if we are to be successful as mothers."

Anita has a vivid imagination. She isn't able to watch horror movies. As a child a horror movie would spook her for the rest of the week. She easily got caught up in things because of her concentration level. And she didn't soon forget the gory details in Hollywood's more frightening productions. But Anita's husband, Bob, was able to remain objective and appraise what he saw. He kept in mind that the movie was only a movie. "It's just a bunch of Hollywood men with makeup on," he would assure the family. "Those things aren't real."

"In reality," says Anita, "it didn't do any good to tell us that, and at the next prayer altar we might hear a prayer such as 'Lord, help the monster not get me.' Now, we filter what our children can watch. We make a list of shows they are allowed to view daily.

"What we watch and listen to and what our children see and hear can be Satan's tool to hurt us. And so what we can legislate and keep from our children, we do. With other unavoidable activities, we try to give them instruction. We teach the children what Satan is trying to do to them and how to handle it through prayer and the Word of God."

A Bible verse in 2 Corinthians 2:11 says, "We are not ignorant of Satan's devices." "I feel that it is very important," says Anita, "for our children to learn the subtleties of Satan. They need to understand that there are many thoughts coming into their minds. They need to know where they originate. They need a realistic picture of Satan and how he works in the world. We tell our children that Satan is not someone in a red suit with a tail and a pitchfork. But rather he's like an angel of light. He comes looking like something wonderful. And only a Christian, with discernment from the Word of God, can recognize him for what he is.

"Along with that realistic perspective on Satan, we teach the children that there is no need to fear Satan. One verse says, 'I have given you power over all the power of the enemy, and nothing shall hurt you,' because 'in Christ' we have the spiritual armor of God. And we want them to know that they are soldiers in God's great army. Our fight is not against flesh and blood, but against spiritually dark powers. Our weapons are not of this earth, either, but are supernatural. Each of our children must learn to put on the armor that God has provided in Ephesians 6:10–18 so that they can confront and defeat the deceiver, Satan.

"When the children come to us with their fears—even if it's through our carelessness in letting them observe Dracula for an hour and a half—we point out that their fears are being stimulated by Satan.

"Another verse that has helped our family is 2 Corinthians 10:3–5:

> For though we walk in the flesh, we do not war according to the flesh, for the weapons of our warfare are not of the flesh, but divinely powerful for the destruction of fortresses. We are destroying speculations and every lofty thing raised up against the knowledge of God, and we are taking every thought captive to the obedience of Christ.

From this verse we try to show the children that they need to capture the fear and replace it with a promise from the

Word of God. For this a good promise might be Psalm 91:10, 11:

> There shall no evil befall thee, neither shall any plague come nigh thy dwelling. For he shall give his angels charge over thee, to keep thee in all thy ways.

"Yes, we believe that our primary tool for teaching the children how to overcome their enemies—the world, the flesh, and the devil—is the Word of God. We major on this book in our home."

From broken home to a happy united family may seem a long road to some people. But Mrs. Bob Green is living proof that as committed believers in the Lord Jesus Christ, "we can do all things through him."

Nine
Joyce Hopping

Years ago Joyce Hopping read a passage from Erich Fromm's *The Art of Loving* which made a great impression on her. Concerning motherly love, he wrote that a mother needs both milk and honey—milk signifying the care and nurture of the child, and honey signifying the sweetness of the mother.

In line with being a good mother Joyce has spent many hours considering how best to prepare her two boys to be godly men. A foremost realization was that she would need a great deal of wisdom. "I knew that there were a lot of books written on children, but I have never found one written on Scott and Matt Hopping." Joyce came to see that the only ones who knew her boys well enough to rear them properly were the Father, the Son and the Holy Spirit. Although she would use good books, her greatest resource was to fall on her knees and cry out to God for help in understanding her children.

"I had an extra problem to face in rearing my children," says Joyce. "As a child I hadn't been a Christian. I didn't

Joyce Hopping previously served on the associate staff of Campus Crusade for Christ and has spoken widely in the southern states (including at the mansion of the governor of Georgia). She is also active in an Atlanta prayer ministry. She and her husband, Michael, a dentist, have two sons and live in Atlanta, Georgia.

realize how seed thoughts in childhood could grow and get a hold on a person. And so as an adult I had a terrific battle sorting through fears and overwhelming emotions that had originated in my childhood years." This motivated Joyce to want to catch flaws in thinking and errors of judgment in her own children in order to spare them emotional trauma and disorientation later in life.

"The question kept running through my mind, Am I going to be thinking through problem areas with them, really seeking God's wisdom for them or will I just be hitting the spots on the surface of their lives, never really seeing their deep and quiet thoughts conform to the Word of God?" In Joyce's opinion, this involved more than teaching the Scriptures to her children. It required getting inside their little minds and finding out where the problems were and what Scriptures and emphasis they needed most.

"Adults often run away from their problems, busying themselves so as not to have time to think. But I knew that as a good mother with plenty of 'milk' to offer I would not only have to contend with my own thoughts, but with the thoughts of two terribly honest little boys. And I have had to face squarely that this will take time with my boys, making them a constant priority."

One summer afternoon God reinforced to Joyce that her family was to be first on her list of responsibilities. A Billy Graham crusade had come to Atlanta, and the Hoppings had invited a neighborhood couple to have dinner with them and then to attend the crusade. It was a Saturday. The house needed thorough cleaning and the meal had to be prepared. The yard work was being done at the same time. As soon as things looked almost spotless, two boys with cut grass on their feet tramped nonchalantly through the house, leaving a mess behind them.

Joyce had pledged to be a good mother that day. But after the third or fourth cleanup after the boys, after the toilet had overflowed, after she realized that she had forgotten to get ingredients for her salad, and after the phone began to ring incessantly, Joyce's nerves were frayed and the boys had an ornery mother to contend with. "So the boys and I sat down to pray. It helped about fifteen minutes," says Joyce, "and then I got frustrated again. I marched into the bedroom alone this time, prayed again, and calmed myself for another thirty minutes."

A few minutes before the neighbors were to arrive, the plumber walked in, and two boys came out of nowhere tracking mud into the house once again. When Joyce put a solemn hand on one boy, he asked, "What's the matter? Can't little kids have dirty feet around here?"

Joyce was about to learn an important lesson. At six the doorbell rang. "I'm sorry," said the man who was to have been their guest, "but my wife isn't feeling well and we won't be able to come to dinner tonight."

"Well," thought Joyce, "what have I done today? I've unnerved myself, upset my children, and turned a lovely Saturday into something of a circus. In short, I have stepped over my family to help some people I barely know, and who God knew weren't coming anyway." It made Joyce stop again to think what priorities God had given her. "Was it right to insist that on a lovely Saturday afternoon my children weren't to have any fun so that I could have a banquet to inspire company?" That night as Joyce went to bed she had a small son's voice of disappointment on her mind. "Mother," he said with disturbed eyes, "you sure were cranky today!"

One problem that confronts all parents is how to discipline a child and to what extent. Joyce had observed that in strict Christian homes, the children often rebelled against Christianity and went their own way. But Joyce also had the biblical admonition to "beat the child with a rod" in order to spare his soul. Through being sensitive to the Lord's guidance in her life, and through being attentive to the Word of God, Joyce came to some conclusions about discipline.

The first was a realization that what happened in many of the homes where the children rebelled was that the letter of the law was practiced rather than the spirit of the law. Many parents failed to communicate in word or deed the intent of discipline. "We are spanking you because we love you and want your life to have character."

Information also came to Joyce through a quote from Susanna Wesley. Susanna lived two centuries ago and turned out two of that generation's most dedicated ministers of the gospel, Charles and John Wesley. She was mother of nineteen and had an interesting philosophy of rearing children. Her remark was, "The child who refuses to go to bed at night is the same child that refuses to learn Scriptures and follow the Lord. And just as surely as I'd see that that child went to bed, I'd see that that child came to God." This was encouraging to Joyce and helped put into perspective her responsibility before the Lord. Bringing a child to God is a job for the parents. They must discipline him, if necessary, to see that it is done.

The next information that Mike and Joyce Hopping received on discipline came through a pamphlet. The pamphlet is titled *Children—Fun or Frenzy?* by Mr. and Mrs. Al Fabrizio. In the pamphlet Joyce read that the biblical perspective of rearing children is to *train* as well as *teach.* To train, according to the dictionary, means: "to mold the character, instruct by exercises, drill, to make obedient, to put or point in an exact direction, to prepare for a contest."

"We realized that to train up a child is to produce built-in responses in him, not just to provide theological teaching. Creating attitudes and character in a child comes from consistent discipline."

The next thing Joyce read in the area of discipline was *Competent to Counsel.* In this book Jay Adams explains that children who are disciplined should know what is regarded as an offense and what its consequences will be before the rule is broken. This will limit the hassle with a child when the offense is committed. The child cannot say, "I didn't know it was wrong. You're being unfair." The offense and consequence have already been clearly defined. And so, on her refrigerator Joyce posted her list: Offense—talking back to mother; consequences—ten licks. Offense—failing to get chores done; consequences—loss of allowance for the week.

"This procedure has kept family backtalk about discipline to a minimum."

Soon after the list of offenses and consequences went up at the Hopping home, one of the boys neglected to clean up his room. When confronted he blurted out, "But, gee, Mom, I didn't know." Though this argument may have worked previously in getting a negligent son off the hook, Joyce now turned him to see, less than five feet away, a list of responsibilities and painful judgment that awaited the offender.

"The hard part," says Joyce, "is carrying through on the promise of a licking for misbehavior. I was relieved to find that if I stuck with their disciplining of certain offenses long enough, the boys usually developed a pattern of good responses. Then we rarely had problems with those areas. Mike and I realized that character training, just like toilet training or good eating habits, would pay off."

In the matter of discipline, Matthew at the age of six had a problem with stealing, as many young children do. He had been disciplined, but still had the problem. "Mommy," he cried one night, "I think I am going to be a thief. I've been taking things since I was a kid."

Through prayer and counsel the Hoppings learned that their failure in training Matt in this area was not a failure to discipline for the offense of stealing, but a failure to discipline the attitudes and actions that led up to the offense. For instance, Matthew would get by without doing what he was told. They were not diligent enough to carry through in seeing that he drank his milk as he was asked, kept his room clean as he was told to do, or carried out the garbage when it was his assigned task. As a result, Matthew soon learned that he could get away with many things. And his little mind reasoned that he could get by with stealing too.

After some time of bearing down on the everyday activities of Matt, a happy little boy remarked one night, "Mom, I'm not stealing anymore. I guess I'm going to be all right now."

"Foolishness is bound in the heart of a child," says the book of Proverbs, "but the rod of correction shall drive it far from him."

"You can be sure that if you tolerate a flaw in a child, it will remain. A child, unlike an adult, does not have the wisdom to see the end from the beginning nor to produce his own self-control. This is up to the parent."

Primary in the Hopping home is the challenge not just of enforcing actions, but attitudes. The children are disciplined for resentment, for pouting, for negative attitudes. They are often reminded, "If you don't do your task with cheerfulness, you have not done the task as we have asked."

"We have taken this perspective on disciplining and training attitudes because we believe the emphasis in Scriptures is on what we *are*, not what we *do*. Actually, I believe many parents fail to train a child in regard to the right spirit. Perhaps this is why so many grow up to *sit* in church, but are *separated* from God in their hearts. Or perhaps it's why so many young people leave Christianity altogether. It's just a system of actions and activities rather than two spirits—God's and their own—being joined together in harmony."

The example the Hoppings use in disciplining is this: "We try to discipline our children as we know the Lord disciplines us." After the session of discipline the Hoppings take the child on their knee, or talk with him on his bed, reminding him of the reason for discipline. Love is behind it. "If I didn't love you so much, son," Mike would say, "I wouldn't take the time to get out the stick."

Through the book *Competent to Counsel,* God also gave Joyce the idea of family conferences. These are not the same as devotions, but rather serve as an opportunity for family discussions. They provide recurring situations where projects can be worked on together and family issues can be discussed. The idea is to talk about potential problems before they come up.

Two things are important for such conferences. They should be scheduled at a time after chores are done and family members can loosen up. They should be held in a place where the family is not used to having other family activities (in the kitchen, minds automatically turn to food; in the TV room, little eyes keep glancing at the set, wishing they were watching it instead of discussing things). Mike may begin such sessions by asking, "Okay, boys what's bothering you?" Or at other times he may ask them to share all the things that are good about their lives.

One time when the Hoppings were planning to move out of their own home into an apartment, the move was discussed at the family conference table. "Now, boys," said Mike, "we're going to have a lot to do. You're going to have to help your mother pack after school and be responsible for your own room. We're all going to be tired and that means we may get cranky and be on each other's nerves. So I want us all to make a special effort to help each other."

This mental preparation was an encouragement to the boys that their help and good attitudes were needed. It also let them know about possible problems that were ahead and what was expected of them.

"Children today are often in a strait between two problems," says Joyce. "They come to their parents with a question and the parent says, 'What are you? Stupid? You should know the answer to that.' And if they don't ask the parent and end up making a mistake, the parent screams, 'Well, if you didn't know, for Pete's sake, why didn't you ask?'

"I wonder how many illegitimate babies, crimes, and other unfortunate problems are the result of parents' failing to look ahead, foresee possible problems, and sit down with the child to explain situations to them clearly." Preventing potential family and personal mishaps, giving the child opportunity to open up about himself, and relaying pertinent information to the children are some of the goals of the Hoppings' twice-weekly family conferences.

Another area that the Hoppings faced was how to instruct their children in the Scriptures. They realized first of all that the job lay squarely with them. Further, the teaching had to be so clear that it could be passed on continuously for generations. This is commanded in the 78th Psalm.

Joyce and Mike practice two predominant methods of teaching the Scriptures. First, the children learn categorical teaching, beginning with Christian basics so that the child can have a thorough background of God's plan and purposes.

Teaching, according to Isaiah 28, is built on imparting small bits of information often: "For precept must be upon precept; line upon line; here a little and there a little." Teaching a child is always built on what has gone before. Therefore each concept must be clearly in the child's mind so that a good foundation is laid for further teaching.

Along with categorical teachings the Hoppings present "on the spot" teaching—that is, seizing appropriate opportunities to point to in biblical principle. For example, when one of the boys had trouble with a bad attitude, the family sat down and discussed what God required in keeping a good attitude. And when one of the boys was not industrious at school, principles of perseverance and hard work were related to him from the Scriptures. "Parents should never be afraid of repetition, for a child needs to hear over and over again the teachings of Scriptures until they become part of his life."

Joyce also asked God for ideas on how to get her kids into the Scriptures. One way to get a child accustomed to searching the Scriptures on his own is when a problem comes up in his life. The parent should write down a list of verses and passages for the child to look up himself. After he has done his homework of writing out the verses and passages, his parents can help him relate them to his problem.

As an example, Scott, the older, was confronted with a problem at school. His father explained to him that some people act like fools and some act like wise men. He encouraged his son to choose to act as a wise man in the situation. For Scott's homework, Dad gave him an assignment (from the Proverbs in the Bible) to list all the things that characterize a fool. When the research was done, Scott had a list which included verses such as, "A fool refuses to accept corrections," "A fool is lazy," "A fool is without honor," and "Wisdom has no place in a fool's life." These and other verses helped cement a lesson in the boy's mind.

"This practice is done with a look to the future, hopeful that the child will become accustomed to turning to the Scriptures for answers to the problems in his life."

Another question Joyce asked God was for ideas in teaching Scripture memory to her children. And so one day while she and Mike were on a short vacation, as she was in prayer about how to help the kids with their memory verses, a creative idea came to her.

"The idea must seem a simple one to most people, but for me it was a breakthrough." It was the idea to have the boys learn two or three verses each morning and to recite them to the babysitter. Then they would each get a card with a clue on it reading something like:

> A tisket, a tasket.
> You'll find another
> note under your basket!

There the boys would discover another note which would lead them to another clue until finally, at the end, came a treat.

With this motivation, according to the sitter, there was no trouble at all in getting them to memorize Scripture.

"It amazed me," Joyce said, "that in an hour-and-a-half God brought into my mind forty riddles to give the kids lots of excitement and fun in their venture of Scripture memory."

And then God gave Joyce another idea. It was to have two mobiles above their kitchen table, one for Scott and one for Matt. After the children memorize their verses, they take their crayons and write them on bright construction paper, then hang them from their mobile with multicolored yarn. "God gave us other ideas for Scripture memory too, such as memorizing as a family, each reciting until all have learned the verse." And there are special prizes such as giving the Hopping boys a trip to Six Flags or Disney World, as a reward for their memorizing a particular passage.

One concept Joyce feels strongly about, and which is making a big difference in her own children, is a mother's prayer for her child—that is talking to God about every area in the child's life as well as her own. "I have found that a list with each child's needs and problems listed separately in a notebook is helpful. I even have a list of goals for the children to pray about regularly."

For example, her younger son, Matt, is learning to handle his money, keep a budget, tithe, and save. He is only eight and so the lessons are at an elementary level, but in line with the instruction Joyce is praying for him to learn particular lessons on finances that only God can arrange.

As Joyce was in prayer about her goal of teaching Matt about money, the Lord gave her the idea of having the children take on a project of giving to a Christian orphanage in Pakistan. They had already been doing this on a small monthly basis. But word came that the orphanage desperately needed a water buffalo to give milk for the children. The cost of one buffalo was $125.00. The Hopping children earn only quarters and dimes at a time, but Joyce felt that if they pledged themselves to such a large amount they would see God provide.

And so the boys agreed to help the Pakistani children. Mom offered various jobs to increase their nickel and dime supply. One day Matthew said that he wanted to put two dollars of the money he saved in the fund. The next day, which was a few days before Christmas, Matt received four dollars in the mail. "Boy, Mom," he said, "the Lord gave me back twice as much as I gave him."

"I felt," said Joyce, "that this was a direct answer to my prayer to help Matthew learn about giving to the Lord." It was a thrill to each of the boys when months later they presented a check for $125.00 to help their Christian friends in Pakistan.

Another time Matthew came into the living room crying. His wallet, containing several dollars of his savings, was gone. Since Joyce had prayed about money matters she was convinced that God had a reason for allowing the disappearance, perhaps a lesson for Matthew to learn. "Lord, help Matt to find his wallet," she prayed. Then Joyce remarked to Matt that it was important to thank God ahead of time for the problem and for the answer—whatever it might be.

"But, Mom, I don't want to thank God, I just want my wallet back," said Matt.

So Joyce replied, "Do you remember our Scripture verse for this past week?" The Scripture verse was 1 Thessalonians 5:18—"In everything give thanks, for this is the will of God in Christ Jesus concerning you." Joyce reminded Matt that God might be teaching him a lesson in trusting him for his money supply as well as in giving thanks in all things. "It's not a matter of feeling thankful," reminded Joyce, "but just giving thanks. This gives God an opportunity to work in your situation."

About half an hour later, after intensive searching, Matt left with his dad for a basketball game. Still no wallet had been found. It had been a difficult and tiring day for Joyce and her natural inclination was to rest and read while the house was quiet. But she was impressed by the Lord that something really needed to be done about the wallet. Using James 5:16 as her source, "The effective prayer of a righteous man can accomplish much," Joyce began to pray.

"Lord, you know that Matt has asked you to help him find his wallet. He has thanked you for the situation. And now we've covered the whole house searching for it. I believe it's essential for Matt's sake that you come through for him now. He needs to see your concern for every area of his life."

While Joyce was praying, a thought came to her of a drawer she had neglected to look in. Rising from her knees, she headed straight for the drawer and pulled it out. There lay the wallet with a small boy's precious treasure in it.

When Matt returned, Joyce had wisely left the wallet in plain view on the kitchen table with a note that read, "You see, Matt, the Lord *has* been faithful to you."

"There's great security in praying through every detail of a child's life," says Joyce. "That way you are prepared for many problems because they've literally been committed to the Lord before they've happened. Along with this, I've learned that the first prayer to pray, as I get out pencil and paper in my quiet time with the Lord, is, 'Lord, what should I pray for my children?' and 'How should I pray for my children?' I've learned many things about Scott and Matt, as well as spotted many of their problem areas through prayer."

Among the items in the lengthy list that Joyce covers with the Lord in prayer are subjects such as the school life of the boys, their activities with neighborhood children, their participation in sports, current goals, personal problems, and prayer for their future wives.

In setting goals for their children the Hoppings have a list which includes their becoming men of faith, Bible students, witnesses for Christ: being responsibile, reverent, filled with concern for others, having disciplined godly attitudes, making use of their gifts, etc. "It wasn't too hard to think of the list I wanted," said Joyce, "but when I thought about how to implement them into my boys' lives the task looked overwhelming.

"First, I decided to work faithfully on just one goal at a time. That helped cut it down to size. I realized that I myself would need to work very hard to provide a good atmosphere, proper teaching opportunities, right perspectives, and the like. But also in prayer I could trust God to work inside the boys, creating the right attitude, the motivation, and giving encouragement or needed testing through situations and events I had no control over."

When it got down to praying that her boys be men of faith, the Lord showed Joyce that faith came through trials. "Along with prayers on this, I knew I had to ask myself if I would be willing to be tested along with my children in order to instill this virtue of faith in them. I consented, and the Lord—with his sense of humor—has brought many trials our way!"

One summer afternoon the boys and Joyce were returning from a swim time at a conference grounds. They were just leaving for home when Mrs. Hopping realized she had left the chicken cooking on her stove at a high temperature for more than four hours. "As is our custom, I turned to one of the boys and said, 'We need to pray for our house, that God will spare it and that Mother will know whether to call someone for help, or hurry on home!' " Scott led in prayer for protection and wisdom. Joyce decided to stop the car and phone a neighbor.

Two days later when the insurance man estimated the smoke damage, he remarked, "It's a miracle that this house didn't burn to the ground. In fact two houses burned down this very week from a similar cause in a much shorter time."

Another time Joyce and the boys needed to take Chocolate Drop, their Siamese cat, to the vet. Chocolate Drop must have sensed it because she immediately did her disappearing act. After thoroughly searching for the cat in all of her favorite cubbyholes, Joyce was reminded that here was an opportunity to test God in front of the children. Holding hands by the car, each boy asked God to bring Chocolate Drop to them. As they opened their eyes an innocent looking cat sat at their feet almost begging to go with them to the cat doctor. Again faith was built!

Joyce prayed that God would open up more opportunities for eight- and ten-year-old children to be used. This came in line with the goal she had for developing the children's spiritual gifts.

The first answer came to her in the middle of summer: an idea to have a Halloween party. "This was very unusual because Halloween would be the last thing on my mind in mid-July. But God gave me an idea to have the boys invite neighbors for a fun time. Then at the end of the party we could share the message of Christ with them."

And so Joyce and the boys organized many games and skits for the party, and the children joined in baking party goodies. Scott, the older boy, prepared a short message telling how a child can know Christ. "The results were exciting," said Joyce, "and very encouraging to both the boys."

At about the same time and in response to Joyce's prayers, a friend also invited the boys down for a Halloween party that she was giving for neighborhood children. Again Scott gave the good news of Christ with the result that about half of the neighborhood children prayed to receive Christ. The next opportunity came at Christmas when the same friend had the boys again speak to the children. This time Scott told the Christmas story and Matthew gave his personal testimony, which he had faithfully rehearsed.

"This is all part of thoroughly praying about the goals for your children," says Joyce. "I try to prepray for any of the problems that I can foresee. I pray for interest and enthusiasm in my children, for receptive hearts among the other children, and for a good attitude on my part."

"It's important for a mother in initiating projects like this that she keep a relaxed attitude, that she doesn't put pressure on the children to perform perfectly, and that she gives plenty of encouragement and help in fitting the message into their own little personalities." The result of the Christmas party was that eleven of the neighborhood children signed up for a Bible study, and Scott and Matt began to alternate each month presenting a short Bible study for these new Christians.

"This type of experience shouldn't be unusual in any Christian home," Joyce comments. "We have taught our children that though people have many needs, their relationship to God is most important. He loves them and wants them to know peace and love through Christ. We tell them also that people may look nice on the outside, but we cannot know for sure if their hearts have been cleansed by Christ. 'And how can they know Christ,' we ask, 'if they have not been told about him?'

"In encouraging your child to take part actively in the Christian life, it is important that they get a realistic perspective on some of the problems encountered in witnessing." Having the children see Mom and Dad in various situations is a great help.

The children have often seen Joyce and Mike confront various types of people with the gospel of Christ. At the YMCA the two boys watched their dad talk with a man about his relationship to God. They could see that the man wanted nothing to do with it. He had a hostile attitude toward Mike.

"This was good for the boys to see," said Joyce, "as when they see big, manly professional football players whom their dad has led to the Lord share the transformation that Christ has made in them."

Many times as she tucks each boy into bed, Joyce talks through their problems. She shares experiences she's had when things were difficult, particularly in witnessing experiences where people haven't always responded well. "This sharing with the child can encourage him to turn to God for help and strength. He sees that Mom and Dad have encountered problems similar to his and survived."

With all the details of being a good mother with plenty of "milk" to give, it's easy to overlook the "honey" of being a truly happy person. Developing honey and happiness in Joyce include: coming to a deeper understanding of God's love for her, placing her cares and burdens in the Lord's hands, thanking God for each disappointment, learning to cope with interruption and catastrophe, and enjoying her children.

One fall evening when Joyce was in the kitchen preparing dinner, the boys called her to come watch them jump in the leaves. Joyce's mind was mentally following a schedule which said, "Now is the time to fix the salad." So when two excited boys called, Joyce's first inclination was resistance. It was a great inconvenience around dinner time to be called into the back yard to cheer the boys' latest adventure. "But I'm having to learn that it's not just for my children's sake that I drop my schedule and watch the boys slip and slide through the October leaves. God knows *I* need refreshment in my own soul. And a late dinner is not half so important as a family having a happy mother, a mother with honey as well as milk." So Joyce laid aside her kitchen chores. As she walked outside, she prayed, "God help me to enjoy my boys. Help me genuinely to love being part of the world of a child.

"Neither the tallying nor the scoring is completed concerning whether I'm being a good mother. But I do know this: I have a growing sense of accomplishment and fulfillment. I'm not rearing my children in a way that I can merely look at myself and say, 'I'm just getting the job done!' I believe I can say much more. 'I'm doing my job well, with my whole heart, mental capability, and physical effort—as unto the Lord.'

"And I've learned a great lesson. When you do your job fully, without excuse or halfheartedness, not only are you a good mother but a happy person as well. Relying on God's resources I intend to give my family plenty of milk and honey!"

Ten
Ruth Peale

"Today, with so many articles on rearing children, so many 'experts' to advise parents, and so much talk among themselves, young mothers are almost developing an insecurity in regard to their own motherly instincts. This uncertainty gets transmitted to the children faster than one can imagine—and the child is likely to take advantage of it.

"But," continued the wife of Norman Vincent Peale, "the mother should realize that the greatest tool in rearing children is common sense. Don't do anything that doesn't make sense to *you*. In other words, you should trust your God-given instincts. Of course, a mother needs wisdom—and this is amply found in the Scriptures. And with the Scriptures, prayer, and common sense, there is no need for a mother to feel insecure.

"I think that one of the best things to do for our children is to help them find and believe in their *potentials.*" And to observe her children, successful not only in material and professional achievement, but also in spiritual and mental

---

Ruth Peale is the mother of three. Her husband, Norman Vincent Peale, is pastor of Marble Collegiate Church in New York City. He has written many books, the most widely read one being The Power of Positive Thinking. *Ruth has recently authored* The Adventure of Being a Wife. *The Peales live in Pauling, New York.*

advancement, one might think that Mrs. Peale had a small corner on the market of developing potential.

Margaret, their oldest, is married, with two children. A talented writer, she gives cool leverage to her Presbyterian minister husband who also serves as executive director of an interdenominational work among businessmen.

John, the Peale's second child and only son, received a seminary degree and is an ordained minister. Then he went on to receive a doctorate in philosophy and now is a professor of philosophy at Stratford College in Danville, Virginia.

Elizabeth, their youngest, is happily married to a senior editor of *Reader's Digest*, enjoying many aspects of the publishing world, and especially the entertaining.

And how did Mrs. Peale help her children discover and develop their God-given abilities? "A mother," she explains, "needs to be in the center of her little brood as a stabilizing influence." Her first responsibility among this brood is to create the proper atmosphere: one that Ruth Peale refers to as a "haven of quietness." And in this loving and caring environment the child's true potentials will begin to emerge —without any verbal push from the mother. "At this point a mother should keep silent," she emphasizes.

Second, a mother should study her children to find their God-given abilities: their moods and temperaments; their likes and dislikes; their reactions to various activities and ideas. One child may be a bookworm, very studious. Another child may be full of fun, one who couldn't care less about studying. Another child may have strong leadership ability.

Now suppose that after careful study you find that one son has artistic tendencies but no business qualities. If a mother wants to help this son, she should submerge any projected ambitions of her son's becoming a business executive and open herself to the possibility that he may become an artist. If she fails to do this, she will frustrate herself and her child.

Third, a mother should praise and encourage her children in their true abilities. "You must project to your child that you believe in him and his gifts. This develops confidence in the child, and without confidence no child can succeed."

Encouragement is definitely a quality of Mrs. Peale. She developed this characteristic in her early days of courtship with Norman Vincent Peale. One afternoon while they were out driving, Dr. Peale asked for Ruth's comments on his sermon. Feeling that he was asking for an objective evaluation, Mrs. Peale commented that the beginning of the sermon was very good, but the ending sagged a bit. At that Dr. Peale exclaimed, "I knew I'd never be a preacher." Ruth Peale had to learn right then that if she were going to marry this highly sensitive man she would have to be a constant source of positive encouragement to him. And she has practiced this art on her children to their profit.

But encouragement means different things to each child. To one child it may mean giving extra help with his homework. To another child it may be much verbal praise. Still another child may just need for you to *be there.* Mrs. Peale remembers one occasion in which Margaret had a part in a play at Marble Church. After the performance Margaret told them that as she sat on the stage looking out into the audience everything looked dark, but she saw her mother and father sitting in a faint patch of light. "Every time I looked out across the footlights into the darkness," she said, "I could see both your faces. It gave me a wonderful, warm feeling inside." For Margaret, their being there was primary in achieving her potential.

And finally, Mrs. Peale would remind her children that if their goal was to follow and honor God, they could count on his direction in the pursuit of their highest dreams.

Along with spotting possibilities in a child, instructing him in good manners is essential in his ultimate fulfillment. This came firmly to the Peales's minds through a psychiatrist friend. He explained that a child who has been taught good manners learns what is expected of him in a given situation and learns to handle himself to his advantage. But a child without manners or with bad manners is bewildered. He isn't sure what is expected of him. He keeps on making mistakes and the mistakes cause him to feel rejected and unaccepted. Eventually it may destroy his confidence.

"Of course there is no better way to teach good manners than to have them yourself." This is the quickest way for a child to learn. The Bible is full of helps on this one: show respect for all people; exhibit an attitude of gratefulness; love others and show understanding. "And the emphasis of good manners is on the attitude, not in parroting words or phrases."

Along with teaching good manners to a child, you must teach him responsibility. "Little responsibilities, fully enforced, will result in a sense of responsibility." A child should be required to do certain things and required to do them faithfully. "One thing we have always required of our children is that they be present for morning and evening meals. This, we felt, was essential for family unity. We didn't decide to do this when the children were older and family unity was threatened. This would have perhaps been too late. We required this responsibility from their earliest years and insisted on it—unless a legitimate interruption was agreed upon—right up until they left home."

Another responsibility assigned to each child was to pack one suitcase to last him for an entire trip. This was left entirely to him. If something was forgotten or some essential ran short, the discomfort of the consequence helped to teach him responsibility for the next trip. They learned. "One element about teaching responsibility is that a parent must be sure to carry through, prompting the child—and taking action if necessary—until he has established a good habit pattern of responsibility in that area.

"And when you teach a child responsibility it takes great teamwork between the two parents. This is why it's important for the husband and wife to agree *before* responsibilities are enforced. Teamwork of the two parents is something a home must have if the child is not to feel that he is in the middle. A child will soon learn when he can get something out of the father or out of the mother. And a smart child may try to play the one against the other to get his way."

In the children's last years of high school, each one was put on a budget. They were responsible for their clothes and all activities, in fact, for their total expenses. Margaret always had money left over, but John never had enough for clothes. He did have a great classical record collection, but he wouldn't invest in clothes. "It took great teamwork between my husband and me to keep from giving in when our son needed more funds. We did aid the cause, however, by purchasing shoes and suits for Christmas and birthday gifts. But had we not made an agreement together *before* we launched out on this budget idea, there might have been times when one of us would have come to the aid of one of our youngsters, thereby prolonging their immaturity instead of forcing their responsibility."

One subject that is important in any home is how to treat a child's questions and sometimes his rebellion against spiritual things. Mrs. Peale's suggestions are helpful. "In so many homes today there has been little or no spiritual teaching. Then there are other homes where the teaching has been sincere, but with little relationship to the everyday life of the child.

"Now what happens when these children enter college or university? For the most part they have great difficulty. The spiritually ignorant youth has nothing firm on which to base his life. He usually becomes confirmed in unbelief. The narrowly taught Christian, when confronted with the classroom philosophy, often finds his faith shattered. This is why it is so important to teach a realistic perspective on Christianity, utilizing the whole of Scripture and how it applies in all kinds of human situations.

"For example, in the area of sex, one afternoon our daughter returned home from school having just viewed a movie of the birth of a baby." She was eager with questions, so Mrs. Peale responded by temporarily interrupting her routine and being attentive. "Sex is a part of life, and therefore questions about it should be handled naturally and spontaneously as they arise, rather than forced into an isolated instructional period. Or it is worse yet to put sex into a religious mold where it becomes too sacred to talk about." The Bible has plenty to say about sex, both warnings and principles, and its beauty can be most clearly seen by a young person as it is relayed to them unembarrassedly by two parents who deeply love one another.

"Questions on sex, marriage, death, tragedy, and other areas of life should be encouraged from a child and never looked on as foolish. Neither should a child's questions concerning his faith." Some parents become afraid of losing their child from Christianity to the point that they ignore or stymie his probing, thinking that in this manner they can put an end to his doubts. Mrs. Peale mentioned a certain minister's wife, who, when told by her child that he didn't believe in God, replied, "How foolish! Of course you believe in God!"

But how should a mother handle the questions and statements of her children? First, says Mrs. Peale, a mother shouldn't react emotionally to their questions. Don't be shocked or unnerved. Try to anticipate beforehand some of the questions and attitudes they may express.

Second, encourage the child to talk about what's bothering him. She can say, "Well, this is very interesting. Let's explore it a little bit." "As you listen to them talk, you usually find one of three things: they want answers to give someone on the outside who has aroused a doubt in their minds; or else they really try to test you to see if your faith is well grounded; or they're honestly and sincerely struggling for answers. All three possibilities require patient and careful consideration."

One question children often have difficulty with is this: "Why did Jesus have to die?" It seems that their little minds cannot conceive of a reason strong enough for the Son of God to have to suffer so horribly. The mother need not in this case assume that the child is doomed to unbelief because he cannot grasp its impact. But she perhaps can find analogies closer to home with which to demonstrate this truth at the child's level of understanding.

One mother started with the importance of life and told her child that because life is the greatest thing God granted, giving it up is the greatest proof of love. The child could begin to see that the pain and agony on the Cross was the essence of God's love—Christ, himself, bearing each child's personal sin on the tree. Of course, some things we come to believe only after much prayer and searching, and leaving the child free to question God and his ways may ultimately be the shortest route to personal faith.

If a parent doesn't know the answer to a child's exploring, the only right alternative is to admit ignorance and promise to look for the answer. Or perhaps the child and parent can jointly investigate with a Bible concordance or an appropriate text. "If handled wisely," says Mrs. Peale, "the seemingly disastrous experience of doubting and rebellion can be a mother's greatest opportunity to strengthen a child's faith."

The Peales had a question come up in their home from all the children at once, not over doctrine as such, but over church attendance—a situation that seemed quite serious at the time. At first the three youngsters announced that they no longer wished to attend Sunday school. They would prefer church. Dr. and Mrs. Peale discussed it and decided that this would be acceptable, provided that Mrs. Peale gave the same amount of personal Bible teaching at home to replace the missed instruction.

This situation proved adequate for a while and then one day the children informed the parents that they no longer wished to attend church. This unsettled them a bit, but gaining composure Mrs. Peale suggested, "Well, let's explore this. What is it that you don't like about church?" After some erroneous surface conclusions it was discovered that the real problem wasn't church attendance as such, but that the children disliked having to sit in the minister's pew. It made them feel conspicuous, they all agreed.

Relieved, Dr. and Mrs. Peale gave their permission for their children to sit elsewhere. But the interesting part is that the children were now more conspicuous than ever. Before his sermon, Dr. Peale would look at each child seated in the congregation and give him a big smile. By this little game the congregation always knew where the children were. "And eventually," Mrs. Peale adds, "the children came back to the minister's pew."

There is another great asset at the Peale home: fun! Mrs.

Peale feels privileged to be married to a "very wonderful man—especially so, since he is a man of fun." His imagination and marvelous gift of storytelling add to the family. When the children were small, dinner time was the best time of all. The children and Mrs. Peale used to sit wide-eyed at the table hearing tales of Jake the Snake and his malevolent brother Hake the Snake. Another tale was about Larry, Harry, and Parry who kept a magic airplane in their pocket to fly, at moment's notice, to unusual and intriguing places.

A mother can add her own element of fun in the home by preparing exotic and colorful foods; by arranging stimulating table centerpieces and interesting room decorations. Fresh flowers add jollity as well as beauty. And then there are visits to farms, parks, and other places of interest which excite a child. One winter Mrs. Peale took a simple excursion with her children to the New York City bus terminal, which has the fastest escalator in the world; then to the Statue of Liberty and the Empire State Building. At other times the entire family has enjoyed trips around the world. "But children don't require an elaborate trip to have a good time. A thoughtful mother can make any activity 'fun' for her children.

"But sometimes a jubilant spirit can get out of hand and become quite mischievous," Mrs. Peale added. One summer afternoon, when Margaret and John were about ten and eight, Mrs. Peale was having a rather serious meeting of churchwomen in her Fifth Avenue apartment. The doorbell rang and she was surprised to find the doorman of the building looking very grave. "Mrs. Peale," he said, "a policeman downstairs says that someone is dropping bombs from your apartment windows into the street. Water bombs. And one lady is wet and angry."

Mrs. Peale could feel the craning of necks and raised eyebrows of the women behind her as she listened to the doorman's complaints. After investigation it was confirmed that her children were indeed the culprits. Naturally, they were sternly reprimanded. They had to clean up the debris and pay the lady's cleaning bill out of their allowances. "But I must confess, that behind our stern parental exteriors, we both had a feeling of relief and gratitude that our youngsters did have a sense of fun, even if it was temporarily misguided."

But the most important contribution a parent can make to a child is the gift of example. A parent must strive to *be* what he wants his child to *become.* One of the ways the Peales have taught through example is in the area of prayer. One such prayer was in regard to school.

Even through their college years, the Peales asked their children to let them know the days and hours of school exams. At the time of the test, the Peales would pause and bring their children before God, asking that they have a clear mind and reap the benefits of their study. Mrs. Peale may have wondered at times if the children were learning the lesson, whether they were building into their framework of living the exercise of talking and listening to God in practical matters. One day she received an answer.

It came when Mrs. Peale was asked to speak before a large convention in Florida. Having arrived a day early she called home in the evening to check on things. Before she hung up, Elizabeth asked to talk to her.

"Mother," she asked eagerly, "at what time will you be speaking tomorrow?" That was all Elizabeth wanted to know. Gratefully, Mrs. Peale hung up the phone, knowing the lesson had penetrated. Elizabeth would be praying.

"Being an example is a full-time job," says Mrs. Peale. Few mothers have been successful in being an example for their children without bringing God into their everyday situations —not with the many needs and frustrations we all have. With just the thought of the enormity of the task of rearing sensible, well-adjusted boys and girls, a mother in many cases finds God real and important to her for the first time. And this is to the child's advantage. For the mother who knows a loving, personal, strengthening God is the surest guarantee that her children will find stability and meaning in their own lives.

Eleven
Ruth Graham

The snow had begun to fall weeks before in Montreat, North Carolina. Toboggans were out and snowballs were flying in every direction. The caroling had begun, rich harmonious voices proclaiming the coming of the Savior.

With the schools closed, it would be just a few more days until Dad would return from his magnificent but tiring task and settle down for a few weeks with the family. One morning soon after his welcome arrival, it was announced, "What this house needs is not a store-bought Christmas tree, but a tree we cut from the woods ourselves."

And so, on a briskly cold day, Billy Graham and his five children climbed the Black Mountains in search of a tree. A beautiful white pine became everyone's choice. After a proper chopping ceremony the fifteen-foot pine was transported by ten small hands and two big hands down the hill. Forgotten was the eight-foot ceiling.

Ruth Graham quickly pointed out the error to Billy, to which he blithely replied, "We'll just cut the top off." And what was left on the late afternoon of Christmas Eve was a seven-and-a-half foot stump with sparsely spaced branches and no top.

Ruth Graham and her famous evangelist husband, Billy, have five children. They live in Black Mountain, North Carolina. Ruth has written for Decision, Guideposts, *and other Christian magazines.*

With time running out, Mrs. Graham sped into town and discovered a Christmas Eve discount—a $1.00 special—on the most beautiful tree she had ever seen, complete with gorgeous cones dripping sap from the topmost branches.

That Christmas, as almost every Christmas, when the excitement had cooled and the children were playing with their father in the snow, Mrs. Graham found a few moments to reflect. The Graham children were no different from the rest of the world's offspring. They were young then, with typical children's antics monopolizing their hours.

Today they are grown (only the youngest is still at home), and an older, wiser mother is grateful that she wasn't left to rear them on her own. "The greatest promise in all of the Scriptures," she says, "is the 'I am with you' promise. God guarantees his presence and his help to all those who seek him."

This doesn't mean that Ruth Graham feels she made no mistakes. Not too many years ago, in the midst of a chaotic situation among the children, her youngest daughter remarked, "Mother, the trouble with us children is that you aren't rearing us right!"

In a generation of "Why not?" rather than "Thou shalt not," what mother doesn't feel the pressure of rearing children? Is she to shield them from society's doings and ideas? Send them out to travel on their own? "*Protect* them," says Mrs. Graham. "Protect them as long as you can, while you *prepare* them for what's ahead." She prepared her children by teaching them about the universe and how it functions. She taught absolutes in a relativistic environment. "God's laws are broken at our own peril," she repeatedly instructed the children. "This is why he set them up—to protect us and to insure our happiness."

And she made her instruction applicable to young minds. "Driving down a freeway helps us see the need for dividing lines on the pavement, for speed laws, guard rails, caution lights, and laws about right of way. Flying into or out of a busy airport shows us the need for laws that govern the landing and taking off of the planes. Suppose every driver and every pilot did his own thing, considering it 'right' as long as he was happy. The result would be chaos and danger. You'll be happiest and safest," Mrs. Graham taught her children, "if you live within God's laws."

In a generation where authority is questioned, abused, and flouted, this petite woman discovered a profound paradox in the story of a soldier who approached Christ 2,000 years ago. The soldier immediately recognized that Jesus had authority. After making his request the soldier added, "I know you can perform this, for I also am a man under authority, and I say to this one go, and he goes, and to this one come, and he comes." The soldier was saying that since our Lord was a man *under* authority he would therefore *have* authority.

Mrs. Graham believes that the system for order in the home, established from the time of Adam and Eve, has been —God, husband, wife, children. Doesn't this mean that if we are not *under* the authority of God, we cannot have proper authority *over* those entrusted to us? With a growing number of parents today confessing that they cannot control their children, it seems reasonable to believe that Mrs. Graham has put her finger on one of the answers to youth rebellion. "I believe that my authority over my children will be in direct proportion to God's authority over me. I cannot expect my children to obey me if I am not obeying God."

In the face of the women's liberation movement, Mrs. Graham remains undisturbed about her role as wife and mother. It was at Wheaton College, in Wheaton, Illinois, that Billy Graham first spotted Ruth Bell. "How can she be so pretty and yet so sweet?" he asked a friend. He knew at once that she was the woman whom God had designed for him. It took Ruth a year to arrive at the same conclusion.

Ruth had been set on being a single missionary to Tibet. But whether single or married, she did not consult society's norms for her decision. Ruth's way of making decisions was to seek God's will through prayer and Bible study. This she believed, and still believes, is the route to fulfillment as a woman. "For best results," she tells her three daughters, "follow the instructions of the Maker."

Church, is it outdated? "No," says Mrs. Graham. "We need the church. We are like coals in a fireplace—together we burn merrily, giving out light and warmth. But scatter the coals and the fire dies out." The Graham family regularly attends the local church, which happens to be Presbyterian.

In this complex age the ideal teaching situation is when both parents can help fit the pieces together for their young ones, but this isn't easy with a frequently absentee father. Of course, the Graham children have missed him. A remark such as "I wish Daddy were here" was common.

"As a man of authority," explains Mrs. Graham, "one word of his was enough to spark obedience in the children." But Billy's discipline of the children never dismissed fun. One thing that remains in the Graham children's minds is the way he played games with them before bedtime. One of the most horrifying to Ruth was a game called "Spider." Billy was the spider.

"There stood Bill, waiting to pounce on the children as they rounded the dark and fearsome corner." And at the sight of the gruesome face of their father, his long arms dangling, fingers tightening to seize the victims, the children would run off screaming, delighted in their terror. "Of course," Ruth added, "I was the one who had to get them calmed down for the night.

"A father's role is immensely important, but the woman sets the tone of the home." This fact Ruth backs up with statistics. Of sixty-nine kings who ruled France, only three were loved by their subjects. These three alone had been brought up by their mothers. All of the others were reared by tutors and governesses. Mrs. Graham later found an article describing a survey to determine whether strict or permissive discipline was best in the overall upbringing of a child. The interesting conclusion of the survey was that it didn't make much difference whether a child was reared in a strict or permissive environment, whether he was reared "by the book" or without it. The thing that formed the child's character primarily was the overall atmosphere of the home, especially the attitude of the mother: her attitude toward material things, other people, friends of the children, standards and ideals, and her husband.

One of the best pieces of advice Mrs. Graham has picked up about a woman's attitude toward her husband is this: "A wife's business is not to make her husband good, but to make him happy. You take care of the possible, and leave the impossible to God!"

Kindness is an important attitude in any home. Some time ago, Ned, the Grahams' youngest son, asked, "Is Zsa Zsa Gabor an evil woman?" And before Ruth had the opportunity to tell her son that she hadn't had the pleasure of meeting Miss Gabor, he added, "I mean, Mom, does she get cross?"

"It's easy to hide behind words like nerves or fatigue," says Mrs. Graham, "but when it gets right down to it, ill-temper and unkindness are really the problem." And one gets the feeling while visiting Ruth Graham, even briefly, that kindness is one of her specialties.

Discipline is emphasized in the Graham home as a foundation for happy children, and for the most part it has been delegated to Mrs. Graham. "I made it a point when they were small to try to deal with things as they came up, rather than saying, 'Wait till your daddy comes home.' I didn't think it was fair for him to have to deal with all the petty problems, nor did I want the children in any way to dread their father's return."

Recently someone asked Mrs. Graham what she felt was the best way to correct a child. Her answer was, "Discipline your children as God disciplines his children." In God's dealings with David, Moses, Peter, and other Bible men and women, God's discipline is always with love. He makes sure that the person knows about the offense; he makes clear to us how wrong it really is. Then he adapts the punishment to that one's temperament and to the proportion of the offense. "In other words, he doesn't swat a fly with a sledgehammer. Otherwise we might remember that he whaled the tar out of us, but forget why."

Billy Graham's studious wife (Billy states that she knows

more about the Bible than he does) also discovered from the B..e that God forgives and forgets the offense. At a well-known military school in the East, she reports, the student court administers discipline to a cadet, assigning him so many laps around the field, depending on the nature of the offense. After the punishment is completed, the matter is to be forgotten. Thereafter, if any cadet brings up the matter, reminds him of it, or teases him about it, he too is assigned the same number of laps around the field. "This is good practice for the disciplining of children. Neither the parent nor another child should bring up an offense once it has been dealt with."

A person may wonder what breed of child has emerged from the home on Black Mountain, where Christian principles were faithfully exercised. Are they adjusted? Did they survive the publicity? Have they suffered from the high expectancy pressure that many impose on the Graham children? Have they rebelled against their Christian upbringing?

"We've had our share of problems," Ruth says. "But meeting them as young men and women, you find them very human and definitely Christian: the proof of the pudding being three married daughters, Gigi, Anne, and Bunny (Ruth); a son, Franklin, in college; and a younger son, Ned, who is at home—a golfing and fishing fan like his dad."

But Mrs. Graham takes no credit. "If your child's decisions about life are honoring to God, consider it a miracle. We can do the possible—keep a Christian home, pray, be an example —but we can't do the impossible. If your child honors God, it's a miracle—and miracles are not in our department."

In every facet of life, it is a comfort to know that strength, encouragement, and instruction are available in the Scripture from a God who is acquainted with life and its challenges. In Christ he walked this dusty earth and brought peace. "If you study the life of Jesus," explained Mrs. Graham, "you will discover that our Lord was the oldest of at least seven children. We are given the names of Jesus, James, Joses, Judas, Simon, besides at least two sisters. Joseph, the father of this household, must have died when Jesus was still a youth, for he is not mentioned in Scripture after the episode in the temple when Jesus was twelve. This left Jesus the leader and breadwinner for a family of seven children and a widowed mother." Alexander Whyte, a great Scottish Bible scholar, suggested that one of the reasons Jesus postponed his ministry until he was thirty was that he had these family responsibilities.

This means that Jesus knew from firsthand experience the particular problems of bringing up a family—including inadequate finances, teen-age romances, overcrowded housing, many of the tensions and pressures that are built into any household. Mrs. Graham feels that one verse in the book of Hebrews can have special relevance to mothers: "Seeing that God understands, we come boldly to him in prayer in our time of need."

"Prayer is important to a woman," Ruth explains. "For there are many things we can't do—but God can! I have often thought that the command in the Bible to 'pray without ceasing' can be appreciated more by a busy mother than by anyone else."

One small instance of God's intervening through prayer occurred when Bunny, the youngest daughter, was only six. The Grahams never had a more honest child, or one who was less of a problem, but one day she came home with an umbrella that Bill's secretary had given her. It was no special occasion, no birthday or holiday, and since Bunny had been wanting an umbrella, it was suspected that she had hinted broadly or even asked for it. Questioning brought from Bunny that the umbrella was an outright gift, nothing more.

Two things immediately came to her mother's mind. If this was a lie it had to be nipped in the bud. No Graham children should grow up with any illusions about what constituted truth and falsehood. Yet to accuse Bunny without absolute proof would be worse than to let the lie pass. "This was a problem I felt the Lord had to handle."

In prayer Ruth asked God to give her help where she felt helpless. And that evening as she went up to tuck Bunny in, the little girl lay crying her heart out. "Mommy, I lied to you," she said.

"The Lord had worked where I could not," Ruth explained. "I am convinced that prayer is one of the strongest weapons for the development of character in our children. In our home it has alleviated tension and restored relationships when at my kitchen sink I put prayer to work."

People often ask Mrs. Graham about the most important thing parents can do for their children. In her earlier years, she might have voiced certain rules or regulations as most important. Recently, however, she has gained a new perspective on this question.

It developed a couple of summers ago when their nineteen-year-old son was traveling alone from London through France, Switzerland, Austria, Yugoslavia, Turkey, Greece, and into Jordan, a long and potentially dangerous trip for a young man. One late afternoon as she pondered over the fearful possibilities of his trip, she turned in her Bible to the seventeenth chapter of the book of John to pray a prayer for her son that Jesus prayed for his disciples. Though she had often prayed this prayer on behalf of her five children, she had never before caught the significance of verses 18 and 19. "As you sent me into the world," Christ prayed, "so I send them into the world, and I dedicate myself to you, to meet *their* need for growth in truth and holiness." Mrs. Graham thought to herself, "If Jesus, the Son of God and Savior of the world, needed to pray that prayer of dedication in behalf of his disciples, how much more did I as a parent need to pray it on behalf of my children?

"I realized that as a parent there was nothing more important I could do for my children than to commit *myself* wholeheartedly to God. For if my own heart wasn't right with God, how could I expect my children to be reaping the benefits of a life that pleases him?"

It is Christmas morning. The fire is lit in the gigantic fireplace, and Belshazzar, the Great Pyrenees dog, rests alongside the hearth as though guarding the stockings neatly hung there. Soon the pioneer cabin (made to look so, with rough logs lining the inside walls) welcomes grandmothers and grandfathers, aunts, uncles, and cousins. Then after the stockings are emptied, the family gathers for breakfast which features steaming oyster stew (a tradition Ruth has continued since her own childhood). After breakfast, the gifts under the evergreen are opened.

Then the Book is brought out and the Christmas story begins—but not in the book of Luke, not with the manger scene. This Christmas story begins in Genesis and culminates in the resurrection of Jesus from the dead.

Billy is speaking. "Without the story of sin in the Old Testament, what can the good news of the New Testament say? Without sin, we have no need of a Savior. We cannot separate our joy at Christ's coming from our desperate need for him. Unless we have witnessed the tragedy of man's separation from God through the millennia before Bethlehem, then the birth of a baby in a stable is just that for us, no more."

"Christmas is glorious at our home," says Mrs. Graham, "not because Jesus Christ is the Savior of the world, but because he is our personal Savior. We have seen our sin, and have met the Savior—the baby in the manger who later died on a cross for us all."

Twelve
Evelyn Roberts

"Living with Oral Roberts is not an ordinary life," says Evelyn Roberts. But rearing the four Roberts children, not surprisingly, is a lot like rearing any children anywhere. The hours seem long and difficult and there's not enough time to meet all the challenges. You ask yourself, "Is it worth it?" And as you see fumbling youngsters begin to make life's sure steps, you know the worth of every precious laboring moment you've spent with them. Recently all four of the grown and married Roberts children appeared with Evelyn on Oral's TV show. The family discussion revealed two parents and four offspring, like-minded on the subject of Christ and Christian things.

"But it hasn't been without a struggle," emphasizes Mrs. Roberts. "Perhaps we faced even more difficulties than the average family. One thing that hit our children hard was the persecution Oral underwent when the children were young." Ron, their oldest son, suffered the most. In high school one of his teachers read her class a critical newspaper article about Oral Roberts. When she finished Ron rose to his feet in defense of his dad. He was able to argue for his father in the classroom, yet when he returned home, he fell apart.

Evelyn Roberts is the mother of four children. She and her evangelist husband, Oral, live in Tulsa, Oklahoma. She has written for Abundant Living *magazine.*

The resultant confusion and resentment from that confrontation got the better of him.

And Ron was to undergo more antagonism than that. Though he had much teaching in the Scriptures and a personal commitment to Christ, still he didn't seem ready for the onslaught he was to receive at Stanford University. When some of the professors learned that they had the son of Oral Roberts in their classes, they not only attacked religion in general but divine healing in particular. As a result certain doubts were aroused in Ron. But most of the problems came because of the resentment he felt in being placed in such a situation. One night the telephone rang and Evelyn answered it. "Mother," Ron said, "how can you prove there is a God?"

Evelyn answered, "Son, you can't prove that there is a God. Just tell people what he has done for you. That's the best way to prove it."

But the battle continued. It became so intense for Ron that Oral flew to his side and spent a week with him in Palo Alto, California. "It's hard enough," says Evelyn, "for any child to go through such questioning of his faith. But it's even more difficult if a child doesn't have a parent willing to go to his side and be supportive when he needs it."

The situation was helped but not completely resolved by Oral's trip. Sometime later Ron contracted hepatitis in the army. He called his mom and dad to tell them the doctor's diagnosis. "I'll be down for four months," he reported. When Oral and Evelyn got to him, he had just come out of isolation and was as yellow as a pumpkin. "You know, son," his mother said, "if God gets on this case it doesn't have to take four months to get you well."

So Oral and Evelyn prayed with Ron and also with the doctor. Three weeks after they left, Ron called and told them he was dismissed from the hospital completely well.

"This is what Ron needed," said Evelyn, "to pull him back to his faith in God. We talk about God being a helper, friend, and Savior, but a child and an adult need to hear that God is *their* helper, *their* friend, and *their* personal Savior. It wasn't until Ron saw that God worked miraculously in his *own* life that his faith was restored."

Today Ron is his father's right-hand man of faith and prayer. In fact, recently, after surgery in Honolulu, Oral had intense pain which no amount of medication could remedy. His family prayed and his friends prayed. He called in as much prayer support as he could and the pain grew worse. Finally, after days of intense discomfort, he called Ron, "Son, you must pray for me." The empathy that Ron and his father feel toward each other explains what followed. Ron said, "In the name of Christ, I command the pain to stop now." And as soon as he hung up, Oral got up for the first time in days, walked around, strolled outside, and then came back to report to Evelyn that healing had begun.

To look at the Roberts children now, it's difficult to believe that any of them ever had problems. But Richard Roberts had his own experiences that his parents needed careful wisdom to handle. Richard took a different route than his brother Ron. As a talented singer he sought success in the theater. He appeared in a number of theatrical productions with such stars as Shirley Jones. And he had a mind of his own about how he wanted to spend his life.

One day he snapped, "Dad, get off my back."

"It suddenly occurred to us," said Evelyn, "that maybe we were on his back. And both Oral and I, with some trouble, took our hands off our son and left him to the Lord."

Some time after that, Richard met and fell in love with a young woman from Oral Roberts University. But he found that she wouldn't marry him because "his life wasn't straight with the Lord." The Roberts' prayers were about to be answered. Richard received the jolt he needed. He sincerely gave his life back to God and as a result married Patty. Richard and Patty are well known as the featured singers on the Oral Roberts Television Specials. "This is a lesson," says Evelyn, "in believing God for your children. No matter what the circumstances may look like, God can change things!"

Oral says today that the success of the children is primarily to Evelyn's credit. This is because she is the one who is home with the children most of the time. She calculated at one point that she was seeing Oral only eight days out of a month. And then, she added, she often needed to have an appointment to get his attention. But Oral made it very clear to Evelyn that child rearing and housekeeping were her responsibility. After Oral had supervised the children for one exasperating afternoon he said to Evelyn, "I'll take care of the preaching and spiritual rearing of the children. But, Evelyn, the rest is up to you!"

"At times," says Mrs. Roberts, "Oral did supervise, even the birth of one of them." Oral had been away speaking. Several days before the expected birth of Richard, he called home to explain that the meetings were so successful he couldn't be home for the scheduled arrival. "And so he asked me something that no one but Oral would dare to ask."

"Honey," he said, "I can be home by Thursday. Could you put off having the baby until then?"

"We prayed about it and, sure enough, the baby came minutes before midnight on the day for which we asked the Lord."

Another time when Rebecca was two years old, Evelyn was trying to get her situated into a new crib. The baby had been used to sleeping with the Robertses because of lack of space, and now she couldn't go to sleep unless she was touching someone. Oral thought that Evelyn was spoiling her, so he told Rebecca she was to go to sleep all by herself.

"I shall never forget how our baby sobbed in the darkness," said Evelyn, "until, without Oral's knowing it, I stuck my foot out of the bed and across to her until she could reach my toe." Touching Evelyn's toe, Rebecca was soon fast asleep.

The reason for the crowded housing condition was that for many years the Robertses had no home of their own. Instead, they lived with their children in spare rooms of other families' homes. But even in a crowded and difficult situation Evelyn knew her responsibilities as a mother, and was committed to doing them well. She had been reared in a Christian home and traveled with her father as a young girl. When she was introduced to Oral, she was gracious, even-tempered, attractive, and well versed in the Bible.

And it was the Bible she sought to pour into her children's lives to stabilize them. "If I had to do one thing over again, I would saturate my children even more with the Word of God. For a child can only think about what he has in his mind.

"The world will desperately bid for your child's mind, and you can't stop this. But while they are in your care and under your control, you can build up an arsenal of Scripture and Christian thinking in them that the very gates of hell cannot prevail against. We learned early that Satan was out to get our children, but we were determined that he would not!

"I'm so grateful for Oral's part in instilling the Scriptures. From the time the children could talk, Oral took them on his knees and told them Bible stories. And he had them learn and recite Scripture verses. I can still hear three-year-old Roberta's answer when we asked her, 'Who is Jesus?' 'He is da Savor of da wold,' she would say."

As each child reached his eighth birthday, Oral gave him a Bible. "And now I want you to read a chapter out of your own Bible every day of your life," he instructed. Many times Evelyn has seen the children go to sleep with their Bible cradled in their arms, as they have watched their daddy do.

"In the same way we give our body regular meals, our soul needs regular feeding too. We taught our children to read a portion of God's Word every day. We usually had our devotions at night, but there was no set rule or rigid pattern. I feel that regimented devotions can become commonplace. And the children begin to think about this as just one of the things Mother and Daddy do." Evelyn read a Scripture periodically and kept a promise box on the kitchen table.

But most of all, these parents wanted the children to get to know the Lord on their own. When they would come to Evelyn with a problem, she made it a practice to ask them, "Have you talked with the Lord about this?" Or "Have you searched the Scripture yourself to see what it has to say?" Then the children might pray with her about it.

Church attendance was a must. "It builds good habits in

the children," says Evelyn. Her daughter Rebecca used to say, "You have to be at death's door to miss Sunday school around our house."

One other thing this family knows about, and that is *health.* What some people may not know is that the Robertses are very balanced in their perspective on healing. For one thing, Evelyn believes that doctors are gifted from the Lord. Recently, when Roberta broke her ankle, Evelyn remarked, "I know that God didn't set the bone for her. He had a doctor do that. But God will heal the bone." At the same time that the Robertses see the practicability of medicine and doctors for healing, they know that any type of health problem ultimately rests in the hands of the Lord. Evelyn encourages mothers to take hold of the Lord in regard to their own and their children's health.

Some years ago one of the children was sick while Oral was away on a crusade. When he called home to see how things were, Evelyn said, "I'm glad you called."

"Is something wrong?" he asked.

"Well, not now," she said, "but there was an hour ago."

"Well, tell me about it," said Oral.

"Oh, honey," she said, "I can never thank God enough for this ministry. You've preached that God is a good God. You've told us to resist the devil and not accept what he brings to us. And you've demonstrated that we can expect a miracle. Well, today it really paid off!"

Then she told him which one of their children had been sick. "He had such a pain I thought he would go out of his mind," she said. Evelyn did all she should do, but it wasn't enough. The child was crying at the top of his voice when all at once she knew that this was a trick of the devil to defeat Oral's ministry, to force him to close the crusade and come home. She put her hands on the child and began to talk to the Lord. At this point, Evelyn broke down and began to weep over the phone to Oral. Through the tears she said, "I told the devil to take his hands off God's property—that this, our son, belongs to God, and we are going to have him well and strong."

"What happened then?" Oral asked.

"Oh," she said, "it was a miracle! The pain left and the sickness went out of his body.

"He looked at me and said, 'God did it, God did it.' " Evelyn and the child hugged each other and gave the glory to Christ. And there on the telephone Oral and Evelyn rejoiced.

Evelyn had heard her husband telling people for many years, "You don't know what a great life God has for you. You don't know what a great year he wants to give you. You don't know, because you haven't realized how *good* he is. And you haven't yet learned to resist the devil and believe God."

One night Evelyn had a serious calamity, for which she needed faith. Her own faith was so meager, however, she decided to rely on Oral's instead. It was about three o'clock in the morning and she was suddenly awakened by a noise of someone trying to break into the house. Immediately she was paralyzed with fear. Her first thought was to be quiet lest she waken the children and frighten them. Then she thought of calling the police, but she was too scared to find the number. Her only thought was "If only Oral were here."

Finally she sat up on the bed and asked the Lord to tell Oral they were in danger and have him pray. Within a few minutes she was calm and the noise stopped. She knew that whoever was trying to break in was gone. She went peacefully back to sleep.

In about a week Oral was home and Evelyn told him about someone trying to break in. At that, a smile broke out on his face. "What's so funny?" Evelyn asked, a little perturbed that he was taking it so lightly.

"Evelyn," he said, "was this about three o'clock Wednesday morning?"

"Well, yes," she said, "but how did you know?" Then Oral told Evelyn that at that exact hour he was awakened and was sure that somebody had called him and told him to get up. He turned on the light and searched the room. Finding no one he returned to his bed and sat down. Then a clear picture came to him of the children and Evelyn in danger. He dropped to his knees and prayed, "Lord, send an angel to protect them." Then Oral felt peaceful and went back to sleep.

After he told Evelyn this he said, "Honey, don't you ever be afraid again. God is awake all night long watching over you."

"Oral, please say that again."

"Honey," he said, "don't you ever be afraid again. God is awake all night long watching over you."

"As a wife and mother," Evelyn said, "I know how much day-by-day events can upset a woman. It's easy to get nervous and feel flustered and shaky when a child gets sick or something breaks down. Then you find the car won't run and you're late for an appointment. The bills pile up and you get a call that unnerves you, or a letter with bad news. Your husband has problems on the job. Someone says something that hurts you. You have a headache or backache and you stay awake at night worrying. These are pressures that every mother will have. Yet in all this I've found that God is concerned about me. He has constantly been my helper. My husband has always said that God is a *good* God and I believe it with all my heart."

When Oral and Evelyn married, she asked him if he were one of those preachers who wanted a house full of children. His answer was yes, but he would be satisfied with two. Well, they had four: Rebecca, Ronnie, Richard, and Roberta. Oral remarked later that he couldn't remember making any silly promises like having only two children.

But after they had the children, Evelyn had a difficult decision to make. How much time should she spend traveling with Oral, and how much time with the children? In the early days of their ministry Evelyn traveled with Oral as much as possible. But finally one of the children decided the question for her. After one crusade she returned home to find that little Richard had got hold of the hatchet and chopped off the bedpost. When asked for an explanation, he said, "Well, I told you not to go overseas and you went any-way. So I just thought, 'Okay, if Mother goes overseas, I'll just chop up my bed.' "

"When they're very small, it's not difficult for a mother to travel if she gets adequate help. But the older they get, particularly in the teens, it's a must that a mother be home."

One child that Evelyn had to be home a great deal for was Roberta, the youngest. For it seems no matter how many times she was told that she was loved, Roberta was unconvinced. "Almost every evening she would announce in a loud voice, 'I'm going to bed. Nobody loves me!' "

Perhaps her feelings were agitated by two older brothers who teased her about being a little chubby. But also Roberta was naturally a shy child and didn't make friends easily. There were several ways the Robertses worked on this problem. One was that they would pick Roberta up, go back to her room, and give her the hugs and kisses that she was asking for. Sometimes Evelyn would have to spend long periods of time with her before she was at all satisfied. "This may seem as if we were spoiling her," says Evelyn. "But God delights in pouring out his love to us, and I'm convinced we can't give too much love and assurance of love to any of our children. Giving in to selfish whims is one thing, but supplying needed affection is another. Finally she would go to sleep contented that she was loved, only to return the next night with the same announcement."

Roberta told another part of the story on her father's TV program. She had often heard her dad talk about "seed faith." According to Oral Roberts, seed faith is *giving* in order to get. And when there is a need, Oral suggests that people give a little more of themselves or their means as a demonstration of faith. This concept of seed faith helped Roberta with her shyness. She decided that she needed to begin to open up and watch for other people's needs and to forget about herself. Roberta would give herself and God would honor her by bringing fulfillment and friends to her. In this way she learned to be convinced she was loved. Perhaps this is a good recommendation for a shy child—that a parent help him or her watch for the needs of others.

In helping each child develop, the Robertses have a suggestion. "Let the child learn to make his own decisions and mistakes as early as possible." It was a practice in the Roberts household not to encourage rebellion by laying down a law too strictly. Particularly in the adolescent years a youth doesn't want to be told exactly what to do in every situation. And this is right; God is bringing him to the place where he can think for himself.

When decisions came up in the Roberts home, the parental practice was to give their opinion clearly and then say to the child, "Are you willing to take the responsibility for the decision you will make?" For example, once when a movie came up, Oral read the reviews and said to his daughter, "I've read the reviews and I feel that there are some things in this film that may not be good for you to see. Since it's your money, are you willing to spend it for something that may not be good for you?" X-rated movies were never allowed. Sometimes the children would heed their parents' suggestions. Sometimes they learned the hard way that the movie really hadn't been worth their precious, hard-earned money.

Another time was when Rebecca, in her early teens, wanted to date. Evelyn sat down with Rebecca and explained some of the characteristics of men and women— what can happen to their emotions in certain situations. Then Evelyn asked Rebecca if she felt she was mature enough to take responsibility for the situation. "Oh, mother!" Rebecca exclaimed, "I didn't know things like that could happen!" Rebecca made her own decision to wait a few years before dating.

"If a child does make a mistake," says Evelyn, "it's easier to fail as a young person than as an adult." God lets us make mistakes and learn from them. And a child should have this privilege as well. Perhaps one reason why four Roberts children have ultimately chosen the way of the Lord is that they were not pressed into deciding against their will, but encouraged into thinking and making their own decisions.

In addition to letting a child make his own decisions, it's important that the parent be patient with the child, not pushing him into things too soon. In regard to this, Mrs. Roberts tells a story of a rose.

One day a mother found her five-year-old son with a rosebud in his hands. His tiny fingers were working at the petals, trying to pull them apart. "What are you doing?" she asked.

"Helping God," he replied.

"Helping God?" she questioned.

"Yep. I was opening up the roses for him," her son returned.

We might smile at the little boy's thinking because we know there is one thing we just don't do and that is to go around opening up roses. We have learned from observation that roses bloom on their own when the time is right. You can't rush them. But parents may forget this truth when it comes to their children. They overlook the fact that each child has a built-in pacing toward maturity.

"Patience results from waiting on the Lord, and this waiting on the Lord can come only when parents have fully committed their children to the Lord. I'd always thought I had really committed mine to God," she said, "until Ron went off to the army. I'd prayed, 'Lord, have your way with their lives.'" And she had prayed this for Ron as well. But inwardly Evelyn guessed she was wanting to help the Lord plan Ron's life, and her plans for him didn't include the army.

It wasn't until Evelyn got down on her knees and fully gave Ron and all her children back to the Lord—"I mean really gave them to him"—that she experienced sweet release in her life. The result was that God's plan and timetable were perfect. Ronnie didn't mind the army one bit as much as Evelyn minded it for him. "In fact," she says, "it was the best thing that ever happened to him. You see, I was going around opening up roses, trying to plan things for my children. Yet I needed to learn again to utilize God's blueprint and time clock rather than my own."

Oral had to learn to leave his children to the Lord too. He had it in mind that his daughters would stay with him the rest of their lives. Their oldest child, Rebecca Ann, was married to Marshall Nash in June 1959 in a beautiful garden wedding. Oral had first declared that he wouldn't walk down the aisle and give his daughter away, but he finally consented. With the wedding over, the guests gone and the bride and groom winging away toward their honeymoon, Oral looked at Evelyn and said, "Don't you ever ask me to give another one of my children away. I won't do it!" But he did.

Evelyn is aware that teaching a child is a full-time job. There are so many things a child must understand. For example, a child must understand that his enemy is Satan as well as that Jesus is his friend. Since the two are working on his life, a child can't survive without a proper understanding of the two. A child must have an understanding of his own importance and of how to take care of himself.

One thing that was always stressed at the Roberts home was good nutrition. The children never went off in the morning without a hot breakfast. And regardless of Oral's busy schedule, mealtime occurred regularly every day. Evelyn is a good cook, too. In fact, she tried getting a part-time cook several years ago when Oral was home. But Oral wasn't pleased with the arrangement. He said he'd rather have Evelyn's meat loaf and potatoes any day.

Nutrition is important in any child's proper development. Many problems that are considered emotional, spiritual, and sometimes moral have a root in poor health. We can see it in babies when they become irritable and upset before a nap or mealtime. A wise mother will check for moods and other evidences of a child's not getting the kind of nutrition he needs. Many books are available today which can help a mother with this subject.

And, of course, good nutrition is a must for the mother as well. Many a mother can get too busy and not take time to prepare proper meals for herself. Or through dieting she may skimp on food—her family getting the brunt of it with her bad temper and grouchiness. Evelyn says there are health laws in the Bible as well as spiritual laws; for a successful life both should be heeded.

A mother's spiritual life is a must. She can pass on no more to her children than she has herself. Evelyn talks about creating certain atmospheres in the home for her children. For instance, her daughter Rebecca knew how to create an atmosphere of sleep for her own children. When Marcia was a baby, Rebecca hung a little music box on the side of the baby bed that played Brahms' Lullaby. When Marcia heard the music, she knew it was time to go to sleep. She began to rub her eyes, hunched her body in a little knot, twisted her head from side to side. Then her eyelids would get heavy and she was soon fast asleep for her afternoon nap.

Similarly, Evelyn feels that a mother should create an atmosphere for God. This may consist of having a private time alone with the Lord. When Evelyn does this, she puts on some sacred music—something that ministers to her. Then she gets her Bible and begins reading, deliberately recalling God's goodness to her. She doesn't make it a practice to sit down and list all her problems unless she can cement them with a promise. "It takes good mental gymnastics to learn a positive outlook on life. And this kind of faith God honors."

Of course, when things get hectic and the home gets crowded, as it so frequently does, Evelyn often resorts to her dishes and a moment of quiet communication with God. She asks for his help and focuses again on some of his promises. Because she determined years ago to keep her mind centered on the Lord, it is now a subconscious habit pattern which aids her throughout the day.

Evelyn tells of one lady who wrote about her problems. One letter after another would come with lists of everything wrong with her husband, her children, her circumstances. Finally Evelyn wrote back and said, "It's a good idea to unburden your problems to a friend, but why not take the next step?"

The lady answered, "What next step? This is where I am with my troubles."

Evelyn replied, "If you won't mention any of your problems again in a complaining way, we can share with you how to go to God for positive help. Then instead of being *need-*

centered every day, dragged down deeper into your troubles, you can be *faith*-centered, by first looking to God for all your needs. Next, begin giving to God so that he can multiply it back to you. And then, start expecting miracles to happen. Let your mind center on the truth of expecting great things from God."

"Well," Evelyn reports, "she tried it but came back with another long letter telling me about her problems but in more detail. Then she made the mistake of telling God, 'If you will remove my problems, then I'll take Evelyn's suggestions.' " Evelyn patiently wrote back again and finally after lengthy correspondence the lady began to catch on.

"I can tell," says Evelyn, "that she is more joyful now. She is starting to expect God to do some wonderful things in her life as well as in her family."

Evelyn tells another story of a woman with a drastic set of circumstances. She wrote, "Please pray for me. I have a daughter seriously ill, a son in jail, and another on drugs. My whole family is falling apart and as a result I am nearly out of my mind." As Evelyn talked with her she could feel the torture, fear, and pain.

She said to her, "In the natural world these problems are so big they are beyond you and me. But with God *nothing* is impossible!" Evelyn asked her if she believed this and she said that she did. Then Mrs. Roberts shared with her the idea of creating an atmosphere in which she could feel the presence and love of Jesus. She told her that Jesus' love would fill her and she would have enough left for her children. It seemed that in her own case, her fear had somehow kept the love of Jesus from being able to come through her life to others. When she could begin to set her mind on the promises and the faithfulness of God, she relaxed. God began to secure her heart and she was able to help the lives of her children.

"Recently," says Evelyn, "I have found prayer sweeter than ever before. Prayer opens me up inside, turns me upward toward God and outward toward people."

Evelyn encourages all women to pray, reminding them of

the time Mama Roberts, Oral's mother, said, "Oral, you don't have to know how to pray. All you have to do is open your heart and tell God all about it. He can do the rest."

And Evelyn passed that information on to her children. "Just say it to God as you feel it and mean it. Say, 'Dear God, this is what I feel in my heart' or 'Jesus, I love you,' or 'Jesus, you know all about this,' or 'I thank you for it.' God looks on the heart, and he is always there with you."

On the subject of prayer, Evelyn knows the importance of praying thoroughly and constantly for her children. "It wasn't nearly so difficult a number of years ago as it is now to rear children. I think that if I were a mother today I would double my efforts of getting the Word into my children and give them added prayer support." When asked how she would pray for them, she answered, "I would ask God to put a shield around my children to prevent the snares of the world from overtaking them." And then there's the mother's prayer that Evelyn wrote:

> Dear Lord:
> Give me patience when little hands
> Tug at me with their small demands.
> Give me gentle and smiling eyes,
> Keep my lips from hasty replies.
> Let not weariness, confusion, or noise
> Obscure my vision of life's fleeting joys.
> So when in years to come my house is still,
> No bitter memories its rooms may fill.
>
> Amen.